The Cookbook that Delights Your Taste

Creative Guide to Cooking Eggs, Macaroni, Rice, Pastry, Meat Pies, Bread, and Sweet Dishes

Kevin C. Crowder

EGGS, MACARONI, AND RICE.

Eggs are fit to eat as soon as laid, and the sooner they are used the better. You ascertain if they are fresh with an oonoscope, or by holding them before a light and looking through. There are several ways to preserve eggs, but to do which they must be fresh; as soon as perfectly cold after being laid, they may be preserved. Dissolve gum in water to the consistency of thin mucilage, and with a brush give a coat of it to the eggs; lay them in a box of charcoal dust and keep them in a dry, dark, and cool place. When wanted, they are soaked in cold water for a few minutes, and washed. They are also preserved in hydrate of lime. When boiled hard, let them cool and place them in a dry, cool, and dark place; they will keep for weeks. If wanted warm after that, put them in cold water, set on the fire, and take off when the water is warm.

With Mushrooms.—Cut in strips or fillets four mushrooms, one onion, one clove of garlic, and fry them with two ounces of butter, then add a tablespoonful of flour, stir for about one minute, add also half a pint of broth, same of white wine, boil gently till reduced about one-half, when put in the pan eight or ten hard-boiled eggs cut in dice, or cut the whites only in dice and put in the yolk whole, boil one minute and serve. It makes an excellent dish for breakfast.

With Cheese and Parsley.—Put about two ounces of butter in a saucepan on the fire, and when melted fry in it a tablespoonful of parsley, chopped fine; then add a pinch of nutmeg, salt, pepper, about four ounces of pineapple or Gruyère cheese, grated, and a gill of white wine; stir till the cheese is melted, when you add eight or ten eggs, one after another, stirring the whole time and mixing them with the cheese; serve when done. More cheese may be used, according to taste.

In Fricassée.—Put about half a pound of stale bread with one pint of milk in a saucepan on the fire and boil for two or three minutes, then mash well so as to mix the two together, put back on the fire, stir continually till it makes a rather thin paste, then take off, mix with it six or eight eggs, grated cheese to taste, salt and pepper, put back on the fire, stir, and serve when cooked. Lemon-juice may be sprinkled on just before serving.

A la Lyonnaise.—Chop fine two white onions and fry them with two ounces of butter, then add salt, a pinch of nutmeg, half a pint of broth; boil gently and stir now and then till it turns rather thick, when you add also eight whites of eggs, chopped; give one boil, and serve. Place the eight yolks, whole, all around, and between and alternately a small cake *feuilleté*, and serve warm.

A la Béchamel.—Slice the eggs or cut them in four pieces lengthwise, put them in *Béchamel* sauce, set on a slow fire for two minutes, and serve warm.

Fines Herbes.—Mix well together in a saucepan, and cold, two ounces of butter with a tablespoonful of flour; set on the fire, stir, and when melted thoroughly, add a teaspoonful of parsley and one of chives, chopped fine, salt, pepper, and about a gill of white wine; stir, and boil gently for about five minutes, and turn over hard-boiled eggs in a dish; serve warm. The eggs are served whole, shelled, but not cut.

Piquante-Sauce.—Dish hard-boiled eggs as for *fines herbes*, and turn over them a *piquante sauce*; serve warm. They may be served in the same way with any other sauce.

Stuffed, or à l'Aurore.—Cut six hard-boiled eggs in two lengthwise; take the yolks off the whites; chop them fine with six or eight sprigs of parsley, put both eggs and parsley in a bowl; add salt, pepper, a little nutmeg grated, a piece of the soft part of bread soaked in milk and squeezed, three ounces of butter, mix the whole well. Then with the mixture fill the whites, that is, the place where the yolks were; fill a little more than full, so that all the mixture will go into and upon the twelve halves. Lay in a saucepan a *purée* of spinach or of sorrel, or of any other vegetable, according to taste; lay the halves of eggs on it, the mixture upward; put for ten minutes in the oven, and serve warm.

In Boxes.—Fold note-paper so as to make a kind of square box without a cover; put half an ounce of butter in it with a pinch of chopped parsley; lay it on a gridiron and on a slow fire, break an egg in it, and when nearly done add salt and bread-crumbs, to taste; serve warm when done.

With Cheese.—Prepare as the above; add grated cheese at the same time you add salt and bread-crumbs; finish the cooking, and serve warm.

Au Gratin.—Chop fine six or eight sprigs of parsley, a shallot if handy, or a small onion, half an ounce of the soft part of bread, an anchovy, and then mix the whole well with two ounces of butter; mix again with two yolks of eggs, place the mixture in a tin dish, place on a slow fire, and when getting rather dry break half a dozen eggs over it, dust with bread-crumbs, season with salt and pepper, and when nearly done spread two yolks of eggs beaten, with a teaspoonful of water over the whole, and serve warm.

With Ham.—Prepare as scrambled eggs with the exception that you put in the pan, at the same time you put in the eggs, four ounces of boiled ham cut in dice. Serve the same.

With Milk, Water, or Cream.—These three names are wrongly applied to eggs in many cook-books; they are creams, and not eggs.

Ham and Eggs.—There are several ways of preparing this good dish; the ham may be raw or boiled; in slices or in dice; mixed with the eggs, or merely served under. Fry the ham slightly, dish it and then turn fried eggs over it; or fry both at the same time, the eggs being whole or scrambled, according to taste.

With Asparagus.—Cut in pieces, about a quarter of an inch long, a gill of the tender part of asparagus, throw it in boiling water with a little salt; boil as directed, and drain. Beat eight eggs just enough to mix the yolks with the whites; put them in a stewpan, season with a pinch of grated nutmeg, salt, and pepper; add also a tablespoonful of warm water, set on a slow fire, stir till they are becoming thick; then add four ounces of butter, stir five minutes longer; add the gill of asparagus; simmer about five minutes longer, and serve.

Boiled.—(*See* Eggs in the Shell.)—Put the eggs in boiling water with a little salt, as near as possible at the first boiling; leave from five to ten minutes; take out and put them immediately in cold water; then shell them without breaking them, and use.

With Brown Butter.—Break gently in a plate or dish, and without breaking the yolks, eight eggs; sprinkle salt and pepper on them. Put two ounces of butter in a frying-pan, and on a good fire; when turning brown subdue the fire. Put also, and at the same time, the same quantity of butter in another frying-pan, and on a good fire, and when hot, place the eggs in without breaking the yolks; then spread over the eggs the brown butter you have in the other; take from the fire when you see the whites becoming hard; put them on a dish, pour on them a tablespoonful of vinegar which you have warmed in the pan after having used the brown butter, and serve.

Fried.—Put half a pound of lard in a frying-pan, and on a good fire; when hot, break gently, one by one (being careful not to break the yolk), the quantity of eggs you can put in the pan without allowing them to adhere together; turn them upside down once with a spoon or skimmer; take from the pan with a skimmer as soon as the white part becomes hard, and serve with fried parsley around.

Scrambled, or Mashed.—Beat six eggs just enough to mix the whites and yolks together; put two ounces of butter in a stewpan, and set on the fire; when melted, take from the fire, add salt, pepper, and a pinch of grated nutmeg, then the eggs, also a tablespoonful of broth; put back on a very slow fire, stir continually till cooked, and serve warm.

Sur le Plat.—Butter the bottom of a crockery or tin dish with two ounces of butter; break into the dish and over the butter, gently and without breaking the yolks, six eggs; sprinkle salt, pepper, and grated nutmeg all over, put the dish on a slow fire, or on warm cinders, and when the white is hard, serve. They must be served in the dish in which they are cooked.

In the Shell.—Bear in mind that some eggs cook quicker than others. Put eggs in boiling water for two minutes, if liked soft or underdone; and three minutes, if liked more done. They are generally served enveloped in a napkin.

In Matelote.—Put a bottle of claret wine in a stewpan and set it on a good fire; add to it two sprigs of parsley, one of thyme, a clove of garlic, a middling-sized onion, a clove, a bay-leaf, salt, and pepper; boil fifteen minutes; then take all the seasonings out and have your wine boiling gently; break one egg in by letting it fall gently in order to have it entire, and then take it out immediately with a skimmer, and place it on a dish; do the same with eight eggs; keep them in a warm (but not hot) place. After which put in the wine, without taking it from the fire, four ounces of butter kneaded with a tablespoonful of flour; boil till reduced to a proper thickness, pour it on the eggs, and serve.

With Onions.—Cut in dice three middling-sized onions and put them in a saucepan with four ounces of butter; set it on a moderate fire and stir now and then till the onions are turning yellow, then sprinkle on them a teaspoonful of flour, salt, and pepper; add a pint of warm water and boil gently till rather thick, but not too much so. Put into the saucepan half a dozen hard-boiled eggs cut in four pieces each, lengthwise, boil gently two or three minutes longer, and serve warm.

With Green Peas.—Proceed as for eggs with asparagus, except that you boil a gill of peas instead of asparagus; prepare and serve in the same way.

With Cauliflowers.—Blanch the cauliflowers and proceed as for the above. Eggs are prepared as above, with celery, lettuce, etc.

A la Tripe.—Proceed exactly the same as for eggs with onions, except that you use milk or broth instead of water.

A la Neige, or Floating Island.—Beat four (or more) whites of eggs to a stiff froth. Put in a tin saucepan one pint of milk and one ounce of sugar, set on the fire, and as soon as it rises put lumps of the whites into it with a skimmer, turn the lumps over after having been in about half a minute, leave them in another half minute, take them off with a skimmer also, place them on a sieve to allow the milk that may be around the lumps to drop. Put in a tin saucepan four yolks of eggs, two ounces of sugar, and mix well; add the milk that has been used to cook the whites, after having strained it, and mix again. Set on the fire, stir, give one boil, take off, add a few drops of essence to flavor; turn into a dish; place the lumps of whites gently on the liquor and they will float, and serve cold. If the liquor is desired thicker, use only half of the milk.

To poach Eggs.—Set cold water on the fire in a frying-pan, with salt and vinegar in it, a tablespoonful of vinegar to a quart of water. As soon as it boils, break a fresh egg in the water or in a small plate, and slide it gently into the water. Then with a skimmer turn the white gently and by degrees over the yolk, so as to envelop the latter in the former, giving the eggs an elongated shape. They may be poached hard or soft—hard when the yolk is cooked hard; soft when the yolk is still in a soft state.

Fondue of Eggs.—Beat well six eggs, and put them in a stewpan with two ounces of *Gruyère*, well grated, and about one ounce of butter; set on a brisk fire, and leave till it becomes rather thick, stirring all the time with a wooden spoon; take from the fire, add pepper, and stir a little; turn over on a warm dish, and serve. This is a very favorite dish in Italy, and also in Switzerland, where it originated.

To beat Whites of Eggs.—Have a convenient basin; break the eggs gently; allow the whites to fall in the basin and retain the yolks in the shell. This is very easily done by breaking the shell about the middle, opening slowly so as to let the white fall, and at the same time retain the yolk in one of the halves of the shell; if some white remains, turn the yolk from one half into the other, and *vice versa,* till the whole of it has fallen. Then add a very small pinch of salt to prevent the curdling of the eggs; commence by beating slowly; beat faster and faster, till they form a stiff froth. They are well beaten when, placing a twenty-five and a ten-cent silver piece on the top, they are firm enough to bear them. If the pieces sink, beat again. Always beat eggs in a cool place, they will rise better and faster. (*See* Egg-beater.)

Basin.—Pay no attention to the old prejudice and belief that metal is not good to beat eggs in. The best and easiest for family use, in which one as well as a dozen whites of eggs can be easily whisked, is of block-tin, and can be made by any tinsmith. It has the shape of an ordinary goblet or tumbler if the foot is cut off, the bottom being round. Size: six inches deep from the centre of the bottom to the top; eight inches in diameter at the top, and only six inches in diameter where the bottom commences (or five inches from the top); the basin being broader at the top than at the bottom, and the bottom being one inch deeper in the centre than on the sides.

Omelets—how to beat the Eggs.—Break in a bowl the quantity of eggs you want, or as many as there are persons at the table; beat them well with salt and pepper, by means of a fork. A little grated nutmeg may be added, if liked. The adding of milk to the eggs makes the omelet soft.

To make it.—Always have a brisk fire to make an omelet; the quicker it is made the better, and the less butter it requires. If possible, have a frying-pan to make omelets only in; keep it in a clean place and never wash it if you can help it; by warming it a little before making the omelets and wiping it with a coarse towel, you can keep it as clean as can be without washing. To wash it causes the omelet to adhere to it while cooking, and injures its appearance. Commence by beating the eggs, then put the butter in the frying-pan, about two ounces for eight eggs; set on the fire and toss gently to melt the butter as evenly and as quickly as possible, else some of it will get black before the whole is melted. As soon as melted, turn the beaten eggs in, and stir and move continually with a fork or knife, so as to cook the whole as nearly as possible at the same time. If some part of the omelet sticks to the pan, add a little butter, and raise that part with a knife so as to allow the butter to run under it, and prevent it from sticking again. It must be done quickly, and without taking the pan from the fire. When cooked according to taste, soft or hard, fold, dish, and serve warm.

It is *folded* in this way: run the knife or fork under one part of the omelet, on the side nearest to the handle of the pan, and turn that part over the other part of the omelet, so as to double it or nearly so; then have an oval dish in your left hand, take hold of the frying-pan with the right hand, the thumb upward instead of the fingers, as is generally the case in taking hold of a pan, incline the dish by raising the left side, place the edge of the pan (the one opposite to the handle) on the edge of the dish, turn it upside down— and you have the omelet on the dish, doubled up and sightly. Cooks do not succeed in turning out a decent omelet generally, because they cook it too much, turn it upside down in the pan, or because they do not know how to handle the pan.

In holding the pan as it is generally and naturally held, that is, with the palm of the hand resting on the upper side of the handle, it is impossible for anybody, cook or other, to dish the omelet properly without extraordinary efforts; while by resting the thumb on the upper part of the handle, the fingers under it, the little finger being the nearest to the pan, it is only necessary to move the right hand from right to left, describing a circle and twisting the wrist, so that, when the pan is turned upside down, the fingers are up instead of downward, as they were when taking hold of the pan.

An omelet is called soft if, when you commence to fold, only about two-thirds of the eggs are solidified; and hard, when nearly the whole of the eggs are solidified. With a good fire it takes only about four minutes to make an omelet.

By following our directions carefully, it will be very easy to make an omelet, and make it well and sightly, even the first time, and will be child's play to make one after a few days' practice.

With Apples.—Peel two or three apples, cut them in thin, round slices, fry them with a little butter, and take them from the pan; then put a little more butter in the pan, and when hot, pour in it six beaten eggs, in which you have mixed the slices of apples; cook, dish, and serve as directed above.

With Asparagus.—Cut the eatable part of the asparagus half an inch in length, throw them in boiling water with a little salt, drain them when cooked, and chop them fine; beat them with eggs and a little milk; have hot butter in a frying-pan on a good fire; pour the eggs in, tossing continually till done, and serve on a dish as directed.

With Bacon.—Put two ounces of butter in a frying-pan; when melted, add two ounces of bacon cut in dice; when turning brown and very hot, pour in eight eggs, beaten as directed above; toss the pan nearly all the time till done, and serve as directed.

Au naturel.—Beat five eggs, with salt and pepper, as directed. Put about an ounce of butter in a frying-pan on the fire, and when melted, turn the eggs in; cook, dish, and serve as directed.

Aux Fines Herbes.—Proceed as for *au naturel* in every particular, except that you beat with the eggs a tablespoonful of chopped parsley, or parsley and chives, when handy; cook, dish, and serve in the same way.

Célestine.—Beat eight eggs as directed. Dip the point of a small kitchen knife in water and cut with it little lumps of butter the size of a pea and of any shape; about two ounces of it, drop them in the eggs and beat a little to mix, then melt butter in a frying-pan and cook, dish, and serve as directed.

In the Oven.—When the omelet *au naturel* or *Célestine* is cooked enough to commence folding, put the frying-pan in a quick oven for about one minute and serve. The omelet swells and does not need folding, but if it gains in bulk, it loses in taste.

Jardinière.—Chop fine, parsley, chives, onions, shallots, a few leaves of sorrel, and a few sprigs of chervil; beat and mix the whole well with beaten eggs; cook, dish, and serve as directed. It requires a little more butter than if made with eggs only.

With Cheese.—Grate some pine-apple or *Gruyère* cheese, about two ounces to four or five eggs, and mix and beat it with the eggs; then make the omelet as directed.

With Kidney.—*Sauté* as directed, till about half done, part of a beef or calf's kidney, or one sheep's kidney, and mix it with beaten eggs. Cook and serve as directed. It makes an excellent dish for breakfast. The kidney may be cooked till done, and when the omelet is to be folded in the pan, put five or six tablespoonfuls of the kidney on the middle of the omelet, fold, dish, and serve as directed. When dished, none of the kidney is seen, being under the omelet.

With Mushrooms.—Cut mushrooms in pieces, and mix them, with beaten eggs; then cook and serve them as directed. This also makes an excellent dish for breakfast, especially if made with fresh mushrooms.

With Sorrel.—Make an omelet *au naturel* or *Célestine*, and serve it on a *purée* of sorrel. The same may be served on a *purée* of tomatoes or onions.

With Lobster.—Cut two ounces of boiled lobster in small dice, mix it well with beaten eggs, and cook and serve as directed.

With Sugar.—Mix well the yolks of eight eggs with two ounces of fine white sugar and a pinch of salt, and beat well the whites; then mix well yolks, whites, and the rind of half a lemon, having the latter chopped very fine. Put four ounces of butter in a frying-pan, and set it on the fire; when melted, pour the eggs in, and toss and stir as directed. Then dust a dish with fine white sugar, put the omelet on, then dust again the upper side with the same; have ready a red-hot shovel, or any other flat piece of iron, pass it over the top of the omelet, so as to color it while melting the sugar, and serve warm. The whole process must be performed quickly. The sugar may be beaten with the eggs whole; both ways are good; it is only a question of taste.

With Rum.—Make an omelet with sugar as above, and when on the table, pour a gill or so of rum on it, set fire to it, and let it burn as long as it can, taking slowly but continually with a silver spoon the rum from the sides, and pouring it on the middle while it is burning, and until it dies out by itself; then eat immediately.

With Truffles.—Slice four ounces of truffles, beat them with six eggs, a little milk, and a little salt and pepper. Put in a frying-pan four ounces of butter, and set it on a good fire; when melted, pour the eggs in, toss almost continually till done, and serve as directed for omelets.

With Ham.—Cut four ounces of ham in small dice, and set it on the fire in a frying-pan with about two ounces of butter; stir, and while the ham is frying, beat six eggs and turn them over the ham in the pan when the latter is fried; stir with a fork, to cook the eggs as quickly as possible; turn the part of the omelet nearest to you over the other part by means of a fork, and serve like an omelet *au naturel.*

With Boiled Ham.—Proceed as for the above in every particular, except that you mix the ham with the eggs after the latter are beaten; put the mixture in the frying-pan, and finish as the above.

With Salt Pork (called omelet au Lard).—Beat half a dozen eggs with a fork. Cut four ounces of salt pork in dice, set it on the fire in a frying-pan, and when nearly fried turn the eggs in; stir, and finish as other omelets. Lean or fat salt pork (according to taste) may be used, or both. If it is all lean, use some butter, otherwise it will burn.

Soufflée.—Put in a bowl four ounces of pulverized sugar with four yolks of eggs; then with a wooden spoon mix well and stir for two minutes; add a few drops of essence to flavor. Beat the whites of four eggs to a stiff froth in another bowl, and when you see that they are beaten enough, turn two tablespoonfuls of the yolks and sugar into them, and while still beating, but not as fast; then turn the rest of the yolks and sugar into the whites, and mix gently with a wooden spoon. Butter a tin or silver dish, turn the mixture into it, smooth or scallop with the back of a knife, dust with sugar, and bake in an oven at about 310°. It takes about twelve minutes to bake.

Another.—Mix well six yolks of eggs with four ounces of sugar; beat the six whites to a stiff froth and mix them with the rest, add some lemon-rind chopped very fine or grated. Put four ounces of butter in a crockery dish, set on a moderate fire, and when the butter is melted pour the eggs in; stir with a fork, and as soon as you see some of the mixture becoming hard, place the dish in a hot oven for about five minutes; take off, dust with sugar, and serve.

Macédoine, or à la Washington.—Make four omelets of four eggs each, one with apples, one with asparagus or sorrel (according to the season), a third with *fines herbes*, and the fourth *au naturel*; you serve them on the same dish, one lapping over the other. It makes a fine as well as a good dish.

This omelet, or rather these omelets, were a favorite dish with the Father of his Country; they were very often served on his table when he had a grand dinner. It is also served with the four following omelets: *au naturel*, with salt pork, *fines herbes*, and with cheese.

With Oysters.—Blanch a dozen oysters, drain, and beat with the eggs, and then proceed as directed.

With Tunny, or any kind of smoked or salt Fish.—Beat the eggs as directed, using little or no salt; then chop the fish fine, mix and beat it with the eggs, and cook as directed. It requires a little more butter than if there were no fish. A few drops of lemon-juice may be added when dished.

With Sweetmeats.—Make an omelet *au naturel*, and when ready to be folded in the pan, place on the middle of it two or three tablespoonfuls of any kind of sweetmeats, then fold and serve.

Omelets are served as *entremets* after the vegetables, and at breakfast. All but four are served as *entremets*, and all are served at breakfast; the four excepted are: with bacon, ham, salt pork, and kidneys. By using different kinds of sweetmeats, an infinite number of omelets can be made, and, except the *soufflée*, they are all made alike.

Macaroni.—This excellent article of food is now as well known here as in Europe. The harder the wheat the better the macaroni. The manufacturers of this country use Michigan flour in preference to any other.

To blanch.—Put about three pints of cold water and a little salt on the fire, and at the first boiling drop half a pound of macaroni into it; boil gently till tender but not soft. It takes about twenty minutes to boil it, according to quality. A little butter, about two ounces, may be added in boiling. As soon as tender, turn it into a colander, and it is ready for use.

Au Gratin.—Blanch the macaroni, and when drained put it on a tin or silver dish, and mix with it a *Béchamel* sauce; add salt, pepper, two or three ounces of butter, a little nutmeg grated, about four ounces of grated cheese, either pine-apple, *Gruyère,* or Parmesan; dust with bread-crumbs, put about eight pieces of butter the size of a hazel-nut here and there on the top, set in a warm but not quick oven till the top turns rather brown, and serve warm as it is, that is, in the dish in which it is. If in a tin dish, put it inside of another dish, and serve.

A l'Italienne.—Blanch half a pound of macaroni and drain it. Put it in a saucepan with four ounces of butter, and mix well by stirring the butter in the warm macaroni. Then add also three or four tablespoonfuls of gravy; mix again half a pint of tomato-sauce and grated cheese, as for *au gratin*; set on the fire, stir, add salt to taste; keep on the fire for about ten minutes, stirring now and then, and serve warm.

Napolitaine.—This is the most expensive way of preparing macaroni. Wealthy Italians have it prepared with beef à la mode gravy only, or gravy made especially for it, with good lean beef cut in dice, and using as many as twelve pounds of meat to make gravy for one pound of macaroni, the meat being prepared as boiled beef afterward, but it can be prepared with ordinary gravy.

Blanch four ounces of macaroni and drain as directed, then put it in a saucepan with two ounces of butter, salt, pepper, a little grated nutmeg, and set on the fire; stir till the butter is melted, and then add grated cheese as directed for *au gratin*, and half a pint of gravy; stir and mix for about ten minutes, and serve. Macaroni requires much butter; the quantity of cheese is according to taste; some put weight for weight of macaroni, butter, and cheese. It is also prepared in a mould (*en timbale*) for *chartreuse*; it is macaroni *Napolitaine,* when every thing is mixed with it; instead of leaving it ten minutes on the fire, put it in the mould, set in the oven for about fifteen minutes, turn over a dish, and serve warm. In using much cheese, the macaroni will preserve the form of the mould when served.

In Croquettes.—Proceed as for rice *croquettes*.

Rice—to boil.—Wash half a pound of rice in water and drain it; put it in a saucepan with one quart of broth taken from the top of the broth-kettle, and before having skimmed off the fat; set on the fire, boil gently for about fifteen minutes, or till rather underdone, and put on a very slow fire to finish the cooking. Water and butter may be used instead of broth. If the broth is absorbed or boiled away before the rice is cooked, add a little more to keep it moist; add salt, pepper, and nutmeg to taste, and it is ready for use.

Another way.—When boiled, place it in a slow oven to dry it, and then pour over it, little by little, stirring the while, four ounces of melted butter.

Another.—Wash half a pound of rice in cold water and drain it. Put it in a saucepan with two quarts of cold water, salt, and the juice of two lemons; boil six minutes, and drain; put it in a saucepan then with about six ounces of melted butter; mix, cover the pan well, and put it in a slow oven for about half an hour; take off and use.

Rice may be boiled in several different ways, or rather with several ingredients. To the above ways, in India or other southern countries, they add, besides salt and nutmeg, a teaspoonful of curry-powder to a pound of rice. In Italy they add slices of ham, sausage, saffron, and even Parmesan cheese. When cooked, chopped truffles may be added at the same time with the butter. Oil is sometimes used instead of butter.

In Border.—When thus prepared, take it with a spoon and place it all around the dish, leaving room in the middle to serve a bird, and then serve warm.

Another way.—When prepared as above, put the rice in a mould for border; the rice must be rather dry and the mould well buttered. Press on it so as to fill the mould well, then put it in an oven at about 350 deg. Fahr. for ten or twelve minutes. Take off, place a dish on the mould, turn it upside down, and remove the mould. The inside of a mould, for border, is plain, but the outside and bottom are scalloped; the bottom makes the top of the rice when served. There is an empty place in the centre to hold a bird.

Cake.—Butter a mould well and then dust it with sugar. Prepare rice as directed for *croquettes*, and instead of spreading it on a dish to cool, fill the mould about two-thirds full with it, and bake in a warm but not quick oven for about half an hour. Serve on a dish. The mould may be prepared with sugar only in this way: put pulverized sugar into the mould, set it on a rather slow fire, and when turning rather brown turn the mould round and round, so as to have it lined all over with sugar; bake as above, turn over a dish, remove the mould, and serve hot or cold, with or without a sauce for puddings.

In Croquettes.—Wash four ounces of rice in cold water and set it on the fire with a pint of milk and the rind of half a lemon; when done or nearly so, the milk may be boiled away or absorbed by the rice; add a little more to keep the rice nearly covered with it. When done, take off and mix with it two tablespoonfuls of sugar, two ounces of butter, two tablespoonfuls of milk, three yolks of eggs, a little pinch of salt, and the same of nutmeg—the latter, if liked. Put back on the fire for one minute, stirring the while. Spread the mixture on a dish and let cool. If the *croquettes* are for *breakfast*, the above may be done the evening previous. When cold, stir the mixture, so as to mix the upper part with the rest that is less dry. Put it in parts on the paste-board, about a tablespoonful for each part. Have bread-crumbs on it, roll each part of the shape you wish, either round, like a small sausage, or flat, or of a chop-shape. Then dip each *croquette* in beaten egg, roll in bread-crumbs again, and fry in hot fat. (*See* FRYING.)

To shape them, roll each part round at first, and with a few bread-crumbs; then with a knife you smooth both ends, while you roll them round with the left hand; the two must be done at the same time. When fried and in the colander, dust with sugar, and serve as warm as possible. *Croquettes* are generally served in pyramid. A napkin may be spread on the platter, and the *croquettes* served on it.

In Fritters.—When a rice-cake is cold, it may be cut in pieces, dipped in batter for fritters, fried (*see* FRYING), dusted with sugar, and served hot.

Soufflé.—Prepare rice as directed for *croquettes*, and when ready to be spread on a dish, add a few drops of essence to flavor; have five whites of eggs beaten to a stiff froth, and mix them gently with it; butter a mould well, fill it two-thirds full with the mixture, dust with sugar and set in a warm but not quick oven, and serve as soon as brown and raised. It takes from fifteen to twenty minutes. If the oven is warmer under the cake than on the top, it would be necessary to place something under the mould, the cake rises better and is lighter. This cake, like every *soufflé*, must be served promptly and before it falls.

With Fruit.—This dish is excellent, sightly, easily made, and can be varied infinitely. The rice is prepared as for *croquettes*, and is used when ready to be spread over a dish to cool. The fruit, if it be *apples, pears, plums*, etc., is stewed. One or several kinds may be used for the same dish. It is served warm or cold, according to taste. Place a layer of stewed fruit on a dish and then a layer of rice over it; another layer of the same or of another stewed fruit, and over it a layer of rice. Place as many layers as you fancy, imitating a pyramid, and you have a fine dish.

Rice-water.—This being often prescribed by doctors against diarrhroea, we will give the receipt for it. See that the rice is clean, but do not wash it. Put one pint of rice in a pan with a quart of cold water, and boil gently till the rice is quite soft or a little overdone; if the water boils away, fill up with cold water so as to have the rice always covered by it. When done, mash it through a colander, put back on the fire, add water to make it thin or thick, according to prescription; as soon as warm, sweeten to taste with sugar or honey, and take cold or warm, also according to prescription.

Nouilles.—Put four tablespoonfuls of flour on the paste-board; make a hole in the middle, and break two eggs in it, add a pinch of salt, and knead well; then roll down to a thickness of one-twelfth of an inch; dust it slightly with flour; cut it in strips about an inch wide; then cut these strips across, so as to make fillets one inch long and one-eighth of an inch broad. Spread the strips on a sieve for half an hour, to dry them a little. Put cold water and a pinch of salt in a saucepan, and set it on the fire; at the first boiling throw the *nouilles* in, boil two minutes, stirring occasionally; drain, throw them in cold water and it is ready for use. It may be kept in cold water half a day. *Nouilles* are used to make soup, and are prepared in the same and every way like macaroni.

SWEET DISHES.

These are served both as *entremets* and *dessert*. Many are *entremets* at a grand dinner, and *dessert* at a family dinner. As the name indicates, sugar is one of the most important of the compounds used to prepare them. It is used in syrup, the making of which is generally more difficult than the rest of the operation.

The *father of cooks*, the great CAREME, divides syrup, or the "cooking of sugar," as he calls it, and as every practitioner has called it since, into six degrees; each one corresponding to the six different states into which the sugar passes, while on the fire, from the time it begins to boil to that when it begins to turn *caramel* or burned.

A copper pan is the best and handiest of all; it can be done in another, but it is more difficult; the sugar turns brown before being thoroughly cooked or reduced. Always use good loaf sugar. If it be necessary to clarify it, do it in the following way: for five pounds of sugar, put the white of an egg in a bowl with half a pint of water, and beat well with an egg-beater; then turn into it nearly three pints of water, stir, put away half a pint of it to be used afterward. Then add to the rest five pounds of sugar, in lumps, set on a rather slow fire, and as soon as it comes to a boil, mix with it the half pint put away, little by little, skimming off carefully the while, and when no more scum gathers on the surface, strain through a towel and commence the working. If the sugar does not require to be clarified, that is, when it is good white sugar, set five pounds of it on the fire, in a copper pan, with nearly two quarts of water, and skim off carefully as soon as the scum gathers. It may be stirred a little to cause the sugar to melt evenly, but as soon as it commences to boil, stop stirring, else it will turn white and stringy. It passes from one state or degree to another in a very short time, and must be watched closely. It is at the *first* degree when, by dipping a piece of wood into it so as to retain a drop of it at the end, and which you touch with another piece of wood—if, by pulling them apart, slowly and immediately, instead of separating it at once, it forms a thread, but that soon breaks. It marks then 34 at the hydrometer. It is at the *second* degree when, by repeating the same process, the kind of thread formed does not break as easily as the first. It marks then 36. It is at the *third* degree when, by dipping a skimmer in it, holding it horizontally and striking it on the pan, then blowing on it, it forms small bubbles. It marks 39 at the hydrometer. It is at the *fourth* degree by trying again with the skimmer after a short time, and when, instead of forming bubbles, it will fly away like threads. It marks then 41. The *fifth* degree is when, by dipping a piece of wood in the sugar and quickly dipping it also in a bowl of cold water, shaking it at the same time and then biting it; if it breaks easily between the teeth, but at the same time is sticky, it has attained the fifth degree, and marks 44. A few boilings more and it is at the *sixth* degree, and by trying in the same way as the preceding one, it will break under the teeth, but will not stick to them. Above 44 the mark is uncertain, the syrup being too thick; it passes from that state to that of *caramel*; is colored, and would burn immediately. When that happens, make burnt sugar with it according to direction.

Apples au Beurre.—Peel and core the apples with a fruit-corer. Cut slices of stale bread about one-quarter of an inch in thickness, and then cut them again of a round shape with a paste-cutter and of the size of the apples. Spread some butter on each slice and place an apple on each also. Butter a bakepan, place the apples and bread in, fill the hole made in the middle of the apple to core it with sugar; place on the top of the sugar and on each a piece of butter the size of a hazel-nut, and set in a warm, but not quick oven. When about half done, fill the hole again with sugar and a pinch of cinnamon, place butter on top as before, and finish the cooking, serve warm. When done, they may be glazed with apple-jelly and put back in the oven for two minutes; the dish is more sightly.

Flambantes.—Lay apples in a saucepan, after being peeled and cored, add sugar to taste, and water enough just to cover them, also a stick of cinnamon, and set on a rather slow fire, and leave till done. Take them from the pan carefully and without breaking them; place them on a tin or silver dish, forming a kind of pyramid or mound; turn the juice over them, dust with sugar, pour good rum all over, set it on fire, and serve immediately and warm. As soon as on fire it is placed on the table, and the host must baste with the rum so as to keep it burning till all the alcohol is exhausted, then serve.

The following cut represents either a dish of apples *flambantes* before being in flames, or apples with rice.

In Fritters.—Peel, core, and cut apples in slices, and then proceed as directed for fritters. Serve hot.

With Wine.—Proceed as for apples *flambantes* in every particular except that you slice the apples, and instead of pouring rum over, you pour Madeira wine, and do not set it on fire.

Meringués.—Peel, quarter, and core half a dozen apples; set them on the fire in a saucepan with two tablespoonfuls of water; stir occasionally till done, then mix with them two or three tablespoonfuls of sugar, and when cold put them on a tin or silver dish; arrange them as a mound on the middle of the dish. Beat three whites of eggs to a stiff froth, and mix three ounces of pulverized sugar with them; spread two thirds of that mixture all over and around the apples, smooth it with a knife; then put the other third in a paper funnel, and by squeezing it out, decorate the dish according to fancy. You may squeeze some small heaps of the mixture here and there, over and around the dish, or squeeze it out all around, giving it a rope-like shape. Dust with sugar, and put in an oven at 250 degrees for twenty to twenty-five minutes. Serve warm in the dish in which it has been baked.

Charlotte.—Peel, quarter, and core six apples; put them in a pan with two tablespoonfuls of water, cinnamon, and stew till done, when add three or four ounces of sugar, mix gently so as not to mash the apples, let cool. Butter a mould well, line it, bottom and sides, with strips of stale bread, about one quarter of an inch thick, one inch broad, and of a proper length for the mould. Fill till about half full with some of the apples, then put a rather thin layer of any kind of sweetmeat on the apples; finish the filling up with apples; cover with pieces of stale bread, bake in an oven at about 340 degrees for about twenty minutes, turn over on a dish, remove the mould, and serve hot.

With Sweetmeats.—Prepare apples *au beurre*, and when ready to be served, fill the hole with any kind of sweetmeats or with currant-jelly. Serve warm.

In Pine-Apple.—Core the apples with a fruit-corer and then peel them with the scalloped knife (the peels are used to make syrup or jelly), place them tastefully on a dish, so that they will form a pyramid, filling the place where the core was with sugar and a little cinnamon; then pour a little apple-syrup on the whole, and bake. When done, pour a little more syrup over, and serve cold or warm.

Apple-Syrup.—Peel, quarter, and core four or six apples, of the pippin variety; cook them well in about a pint of water, a wine-glass of brandy, and a pinch of grated cinnamon; when well cooked, put them in a coarse towel, and press the juice out; put it in a stewpan and set it on a good fire; add a pound of loaf-sugar, take the foam off with a skimmer a little before it boils, and boil about five minutes; take from the fire, let cool, bottle it, corking well. It may be kept for months. Syrup with pears, pine-apple, etc., is made in the same way.

Blanc-Mange.—Set on the fire in a block-tin saucepan one quart of milk with the rind of a lemon and two tablespoonfuls of sugar; stir occasionally to melt the sugar. Then mix about six ounces of corn-starch with half a pint of milk in a bowl. As soon as the milk rises, take it from the fire; take off with a skimmer the rind of lemon, and the skin that has formed on the top of the milk; put the milk back on the fire; turn the corn-starch into it, stir continually and very fast till it is very thick. It will take hardly a minute to get thick. Turn into a mould wetted with cold water and put away to cool. When perfectly cold, serve with the following sauce: Mix well in a tin saucepan two ounces of sugar and two yolks of eggs, then add half a pint of milk and mix again; set on the fire; stir continually, give one boil; take off; let cool, and serve.

Blanc-Manger.—Throw in boiling water two ounces of sweet almonds and the same of bitter ones, or pour boiling water over them, and then skin them as soon as the skin comes off easily. Pound them well with four ounces of sugar, lay the whole in a pan with about a pint of water, set on the fire, and when on the point of boiling, take off and strain. Put in a tin saucepan about a pint of milk, the strained juice, an ounce of gelatin, a little rind of lemon, and a little nutmeg, both grated; set the whole on a moderate fire; simmer just enough to melt the gelatin and mix it with the rest, and then strain. Wet a mould with cold water, put the mixture in it, set it on ice, and serve when cool. It may be served with a sauce like the above.

Charlotte Russe.—Wipe a mould well, see that it is dry, and then line the bottom and sides with lady's-fingers, or sponge cake cut in pieces about the size of a lady's-finger. Commence by lining the bottom, placing the pieces so as to form a star or rosette, or plain, according to fancy. Then place some of them upright all around, rather tight, and even with the top of the mould. Fill with cream, well whipped, sweetened, and flavored with essence; place the mould on ice, and when ready to serve, place a dish on it, turn upside down, remove the mould, and serve as it is, or decorated.

To decorate.—Make a paper funnel, fill it with cream, or icing (sugar and white of egg worked), then spread some all over the top according to fancy; it is quickly done and is sightly. The mould may also be filled with some other cream; as *crème légère, crème cuite,* etc.

Charlotte à la Chantilly.—It is a *Charlotte* made exactly as the above one, but filled with *crème à la Chantilly*.

A la Polonaise.—Make a sponge cake, cut it transversely, dip each piece in cream (any kind) and then place them back where they were so as to give the cake its original form as near as possible. When thus re-formed, cover it with cream, dust with sugar, and decorate with any kind of sweetmeats. Besides the sweetmeats that are placed here and there all around, some currant-jelly may also be used to decorate. Place on ice for some time, and serve.

Italian.—Peel, quarter, and core about a quart of pears and set them on a rather slow fire, in a saucepan with half a pint of white wine, sugar, cinnamon, and lemon-rind. While they are cooking, line a mould as for *Charlotte Russe,* remove the lemon-rind, and fill the mould with the pears; place it on ice when cool, turn over on a dish, remove the mould, decorate with icing, or cover entirely with apple-jelly, and serve. It is also made with *génoise* cake instead of sponge cake.

Française.—This is prepared and served like a *Charlotte Russe*, with the exception that it is filled with *blanc manger* or *fromage à la crème* instead of cream.

Of Fruit.—This is made of cherries or any kind of berries; cherries must be stoned carefully. Dip the fruit in wine-jelly as soon as the latter is cool, but not firm, and line a mould with it. By having the mould on ice it will be more easily done. Fill the mould with cream, as for *Charlotte Russe*, place on ice, and serve as soon as congealed. When the mould is taken from the ice, dip it in warm water a few seconds, place a dish over it, turn upside down, remove it, and serve immediately. A *Charlotte* of fruit is sightly enough without decorations; it requires some time to make it, but it is worth the trouble, being a handsome as well as a good dish.

Another.—Line a mould as for the above. Put one ounce of gelatin in a bowl with about three tablespoonfuls of water and leave it so for about half an hour. Mix well together in a saucepan four yolks of eggs and three ounces of pulverized sugar, add about three tablespoonfuls of milk, and mix again; set on the fire and stir for about three minutes, add the gelatin, stir again, give one boil, and put away to cool a little. Beat four whites of eggs to a stiff froth, turn the above mixture into them, mix gently again; fill the mould with the whole, place on ice till perfectly cold. When cold, turn upside down on a dish, remove the mould, decorate as the preceding one, and serve cold.

Cheese with Cream—(Fromage à la Crème).—This is made in different ways; sometimes with soft curds only, or with curds and cream, or with cream only when very thick. Gelatin dissolved in a little water may also be added. The curds or cream, or both, are beaten with an egg-beater, sweetened to taste with sugar, and flavored with essence. To make it more sightly, when beaten and flavored, it is moulded, placed on ice to make it firm, and then turned over a dish, the mould removed, and then served. Any kind of essence may be used to flavor it, such as vanilla, *fleur d'oranger*, rose-water, violet, etc.; it may also be made with coffee, tea, chocolate, orange, lemon, etc. Put a few drops of very strong coffee, or tea, or chocolate at the same time with the sugar and essence.

With orange or lemon, rub them on a piece of sugar, which you pound and use to sweeten the cheese. Three or more different ones may be made with a quart of curds; for instance, flavor one third of it with essence, another third with coffee or chocolate, and the other with orange. The colors will be different also. It is an excellent and refreshing *entremets* in summer-time. Cheese may also be flavored with pine-apple cut in very small dice and mixed with it instead of essence.

Compotes, or Jams.—How to make syrup for Compotes.—Common Syrup. —Put a pound of loaf-sugar in a crockery stewpan, with a pint of water, a wine-glass of brandy, and a pinch of well-grated cinnamon; set it on a slow fire, boil gently for ten minutes, skimming off the foam; then take from the fire and let cool; bottle it; cork it well and keep it to use when wanted. It may be kept for months in a cool and dry place.

Stewed fruit of any kind is called either *compote* or jam. They are first peeled and cored and then cooked with sugar, water, and sometimes cinnamon, or cloves, both in powder and according to taste; also lemon-juice or rind to taste. Cinnamon agrees well with any kind of apples, but is not liked by every one in every kind of fruit. The fruits may be cooked and served whole, in halves, or quarters, or mashed, according to fancy and taste. The proportions of water and sugar are also according to taste, or according to the nature or state of the fruit. Sour apples require more sugar than sweet ones, unripe berries require more also than ripe ones. The preparation is very simple; not being prepared to keep, they are served as soon as cold. They may be served warm, but they are certainly not as good. When there is not syrup (juice) enough, pour some of the above over the fruit, or some apple-syrup. The peels and cores of the apples may be used to make syrup, together with those of pears.

While peeling, coring, or cutting fruit, drop each in cold water, else it changes color and is unsightly.

When cold, the *compote* may be put in a mould; turn over a dish, remove the mould, and serve. Several kinds may be served on the same dish as well as one; being of different colors, the dish is more sightly, and quite as good. Loaf-sugar is the best.

Instead of cooking them with water, etc., as directed above, put some syrup on the fire, and as soon as it boils, drop the prepared fruit in it, and boil slowly till done.

Of Apples.—Quarter, peel, core, and put apples in a stewpan with a gill of water for two quarts, sugar and cinnamon to taste; when done, dish them, pour the juice in the stewpan all over, and serve cold. If there is not juice enough, add some apple-syrup.

Of Apricots or Peaches.—Take two quarts of apricots or peaches and cut them in two, remove the stones. Throw them in boiling water for two minutes and take off; drop in cold water and take out immediately, then skin them. Put about half a pint of water in a crockery pan or in a well-lined one, and at the first boil put the peaches in, with sugar to taste; boil gently till done, turn the whole over a dish, and serve cold. If there is not juice or syrup enough, add a little common syrup.

Of Blackberries, Currants, Raspberries, Strawberries, and other like Berries.—Prepare syrup of sugar, and when at the second, third, or fourth state, throw the berries in; boil from one to five minutes, according to the kind, take from the fire, and serve when cold.

Of Cherries.—Cut off the stalks of the cherries about half their length, wash well and drain them. Put them in a stewpan in which there is just enough syrup at the first degree to cover them; boil slowly till cooked, and serve.

Of Oranges.—Peel four oranges, and divide each carpel without breaking it, and then throw them in syrup of sugar at the fourth or fifth degree, and boil slowly three or four minutes; take from the fire, let cool, and serve.

Of Pears.—Peel the pears, cut the stem half its length, put them in a stewpan with a little sugar, a few drops of lemon-juice, a pinch of cinnamon, and a little water. Set on a moderate fire, and at the first boiling add two gills of claret wine. Simmer till cooked, then put the pears only on a dish; set the stewpan back on the fire, add to the juice in it about the same quantity of syrup of pears or of syrup of sugar at the third degree, boil fifteen minutes longer, pour the whole on the pears, and serve warm or cold.

Of Lemons.—Peel the lemons, cut them in pieces, remove the seeds, and proceed as for that of oranges, boiling a little longer.

Of Pine-Apple.—Peel and cut in slices, put them in a crockery pan, with a little water and sugar, set on a good fire, and finish and serve like apricots.

Of Plums.—Throw the plums in boiling water, and take them out when half cooked; put them in a crockery stewpan, with a little water and a little sugar; simmer till cooked, place them on a dish, pour some common syrup on, and serve when cold.

Of Quinces.—Quarter, peel, and core the quinces; throw them in boiling water for five minutes; take out and drain them; put them in a crockery stewpan, with four ounces of sugar for every pound of quinces, a few drops of lemon-juice, a little water, and a pinch of grated cinnamon; set it on the fire, simmer till cooked, place them on a dish, pour some common syrup on them, and serve cold.

Of Chestnuts.—Roast about one quart of chestnuts, remove the skin and pith, lay them in a pan with half a gill of water and four ounces of sugar; set on a slow fire, toss now and then till the sugar and water are absorbed or evaporated, turn over a dish, dust with sugar, and serve warm or cold. A few drops of lemon-juice may be added just before dusting with sugar.

Cold Compote.—Wash strawberries and raspberries in cold water, drain dry, and place them on a dish. Pour boiling common syrup or boiling currant-jelly all over; let cool, and serve.

Of Cranberries.—Put one pint of water in a tin saucepan, with six ounces of loaf-sugar, the rind of half a lemon, and set it on the fire; boil down until, by dipping a spoon in it, it adheres to it. Then throw in it about one pint of cranberries; boil about twelve minutes, stirring now and then, take off, let cool, and serve.

Another.—After having boiled ten minutes in the same way as above, and with the same proportions of sugar, cranberries, etc., take from the fire, mash through a fine colander or sieve, put back on the fire, boil gently five minutes, let cool, and serve.

Creams or Crèmes au Citron (with Lemon).—Put one pint of milk in a tin saucepan with the rind of a lemon; set on the fire, and as soon as it rises place an iron spoon in it and boil gently five minutes; take from the fire. Mix well in a bowl four ounces of sugar with four yolks of eggs, then turn the milk into the bowl, little by little, stirring and mixing at the same time. Strain the mixture and put it in small cups; put the cups in a pan of boiling water, boil gently for about ten minutes, and put in the oven as it is, that is, leaving the cups in the water. The cups must not be more than half covered with water, else the water will fly into it. It takes from ten to fifteen minutes to finish the cooking in the oven, according to the size of the cups. Take them from the oven when the *crème* is rather firm, except a little spot in the middle, and which you ascertain by moving the cups.

Anyone with an ordinary amount of intelligence can make creams as well as the best cooks, after having tried only two or three times. When you know how to make one, you can make fifty, just by using different flavorings.

Au Café (with Coffee).—The stronger the coffee the better the cream. The most economical way of making strong coffee is: when you intend to have cream with coffee for dinner, put the first drops that fall, when you make the coffee for breakfast, into a glass; put it immediately in cold water, and as soon as cool cover it with paper, which you tie around it with twine, and use when you make the cream.

Always use good fresh milk and fresh eggs. As soon as the whites of the eggs are separated from the yolks, put them, together with the shells, on ice, and use the next day to clarify your jellies, or to make icing, etc. A little care is a great saving in the kitchen.

Put one quart of milk in a milk-pan on the fire and take off as soon as it rises. While the milk is on the fire, mix well together in a bowl eight yolks of eggs with half a pound of sugar, and coffee to flavor; then turn the milk into the mixture, little by little, stirring the while; when the whole is thoroughly mixed, strain it. Put the mixture in cream-cups, place the cups in a pan of boiling water—enough water to half cover them; boil slowly for about ten minutes, put the pan and cups in a moderately-heated oven, and take off when done. It takes from ten to fifteen minutes to finish the cooking, according to the size of the cups. It is done when the whole is solidified except a little spot in the centre, which, by moving the cups, will shake somewhat. Serve cold.

With Burnt Sugar.—Put two ounces of sugar in a small tin pan, with a tablespoonful of water, set on the fire, and boil till burnt and of a light-brown color; take off, and put it in a stewpan with a pint of milk, four ounces of white sugar, a few drops of rose or orange-flower water; boil ten minutes, stirring occasionally; take from the fire, beat the yolks of two eggs, and one entire, put in the pan and mix the whole well, then strain, after which you put the mixture in small cream-pots for that purpose; place them in a hot but not boiling *bain-marie,* and as soon as it thickens take them out, dust them with fine white sugar, let cool; place them on ice for about fifteen minutes, and then it is ready to be served.

With Chocolate.—Put in a stewpan and on a moderate fire six ounces of chocolate, three tablespoonfuls of water, three ounces of white sugar, stir now and then with a wooden spoon till melted; then pour in it, little by little, a quart of good fresh milk; boil ten minutes, take from the fire, and mix in it one egg well beaten with the yolks of five others; strain through a fine sieve, put in cream-pots or cups, place them in a hot but not boiling *bain-marie,* take off as soon as it thickens, dust with fine white sugar, let cool, place on ice for about fifteen minutes, and use.

With Orange.—Use orange-rind, and proceed as for lemon-cream in every other particular.

With Tea.—Proceed with strong tea as for cream *au café* in every other particular.

With Essence.—Make cream *au café,* with the exception that, instead of using coffee to flavor, you use a few drops of vanilla, rose-water, orange-flower water, violet, cinnamon, etc.—any kind of essence, to taste.

With Cinnamon.—Beat well together in a bowl about an ounce of potato-starch, a teaspoonful of cinnamon, four eggs, four ounces of sugar, and milk enough to make a rather liquid batter. Turn the mixture into a mould, which put into a pan of boiling water for fifteen minutes, then place in the oven till cooked. Serve cold.

Cuite.—Put two ounces of sugar in a tin pan with two eggs, and mix well; then add an ounce of flour, little by little, mixing the while; then, in the same way, add also about a pint of boiled milk; set on the fire, stir continually till it turns rather thick; take off, flavor with essence to taste, let cool, and serve or use for filling.

Frangipane.—Set one pint of milk on the fire. Mix well together in another pan three tablespoonfuls of sugar, two of flour, three eggs, three macaroons crumbled, and as soon as the milk rises, turn the mixture into it, little by little, stirring and mixing the while; keep stirring about three minutes; take off, add a few drops of essence to flavor; turn into a bowl, let cool, and it is ready for use. It may be made without the macaroons.

With Almonds.—Make as the above, with the exception that you use sweet almonds, chopped fine, instead of macaroons.

With Hazel-nuts.—Proceed as above, using hazel-nuts instead of almonds.

Légère.—Mix well together in a tin saucepan five yolks of eggs and five ounces of sugar; add four tablespoonfuls of milk, and mix again. Set the pan on the fire, and stir continually till it turns rather thick; take off, and add a few drops of essence; turn into a plate or dish and let cool. When cold, beat five whites of eggs to a stiff froth; have somebody to pour in the whites, and, while you are still beating, about two tablespoonfuls of the cold mixture, and stop beating. Then turn the rest of the mixture into the whites, and mix the whole together gently; do not stir too much, but move round and round with a wooden spoon, and it is done. If it is stirred too much, it may become too liquid. It makes an excellent and light cream.

Patissière.—Beat four whites of eggs to a stiff froth, and then mix about one ounce of pulverized sugar with them. Put four yolks of egg in a bowl with half a gill of milk, and beat well till thoroughly mixed. Put in a saucepan about two ounces of pulverized sugar, with a teaspoonful of potato-starch (*fecula*), and two-thirds of a gill of milk, and mix the whole well; then add the eggs and milk, and beat the whole well with an egg-beater. Set the pan on a rather slow fire, stir continually with a wooden spoon till it turns rather thick, and then turn the four whites and sugar into the pan also, little by little, stirring the while, and take off when thoroughly mixed. As soon as off the fire, add essence to flavor, and about one-quarter of an ounce of gelatine, dissolved in tepid water. Serve, or use to fill when cold.

Renversée.—Make cream with tea, coffee, or chocolate, and instead of turning the mixture into cream pots, turn it into a mould lined with burnt sugar; place the mould in boiling water for about fifteen minutes, place it in the oven to finish the cooking, turn over a dish, remove the mould, and serve cold. To line the mould, put two or three tablespoonfuls of pulverized sugar in it; set it on a slow fire, and when the sugar is melted and turning brown, move the mould round and round to spread the sugar all over; then put the cream in it.

Sweet Cream.—We mean here the oily substance which forms a scum on milk; also called *whipped cream.* It is used to make Charlotte Russe, to fill *meringues, choux,* or cream-cakes, etc.

Put a pint of good thick cream in a bowl, and if the weather is warm, place the bowl on ice for half an hour, then beat the cream with an egg-beater till stiff and thick. If the cream does not become stiff after having beaten it fifteen or twenty minutes at the longest, it is not good, or it is too warm. Good cream may rise and become stiff in five minutes. When beaten, add to it about four ounces of pulverized sugar, which you mix gently with it, not stirring too much; add also a few drops of essence to flavor. If wanted very stiff, add also, after the sugar, half an ounce of gelatin, melted in a little tepid water. When beaten and mixed, if not used immediately, it must be put on ice.

Chantilly.—It is the above cream flavored with *fleur d'orange* (orange-flower water), or with essence of violet.

Ice Cream.—Made with cream it is richer than with milk. With eggs it is better and richer than without, and those that advocate it without eggs, either have no palate, or do not know how to use them in making it.

The addition of starch, fecula, arrow-root, flour, meal, etc., spoils it. The proportions are, to a quart of milk or cream: from four to six eggs; from eight to fourteen ounces of pulverized sugar; essence, or chocolate, or fruit-jelly to flavor and color. Our receipt is for six eggs and fourteen ounces of sugar to a quart of milk.

Set the milk on the fire, and when it comes to a boil, mix well half the sugar and the essence with six yolks and three whites of eggs; beat the three other whites separately to a stiff froth. As soon as the milk rises, take it from the fire, put half the sugar in it and stir to melt it, then turn the mixture into it also, little by little, beating the while with an egg-beater; set on the fire, and take off at the first boiling. While on the fire it must be beaten gently, as, if it is allowed to boil, the eggs may curdle. As soon as off the fire, mix the three whites with the rest, beating with an egg-beater, just enough to mix the whole well; put in cold, salt water to cool, and then freeze.

The smaller the ice is broken and mixed with plenty of rock-salt, the quicker it freezes.

Custard.—Put four yolks of eggs in a bowl, then sprinkle flour on them, little by little, stirring and mixing well the while with a wooden spoon, and when the mixture is rather thick, stop sprinkling flour, but sprinkle milk, and mix again in the same way till the mixture is liquid; add sugar and essence to taste, beat the four whites to a stiff froth, mix them gently with the rest; butter a mould well, fill it about two-thirds full with the mixture, and set in a warm but not quick oven. Serve as soon as out of the oven. If intended to be served cold, omit the whites of eggs.

Fritters.—These are made with every kind of fruit, when ripe, peeled and stoned, or cored when necessary, and according to the kind. The fruit is used whole, such as strawberries and the like; or in slices, such as apples, pears, etc.; or in halves, like peaches, plums, etc. It may be used as soon as prepared; or may be soaked a few hours in a mixture of sugar, brandy, or rum, and lemon-rind.

Have *batter for fritters* made in advance, and while you are preparing the fruit heat the fat (*see* FRYING), dip each fruit or each slice in batter, drop it in the fat, stir and turn over, and when done, turn into a colander, dust well with fine white or pulverized sugar, and serve as warm (or rather as hot) as possible. Even the best fritters served cold make a very poor dish. Besides fruit, the blossoms of the acacia and those of the violet make the most delicate fritters.

With Bread or Pain perdu.—Set one pint of milk on the fire with two ounces of sugar, and the rind of half a lemon, stir now and then, and when it rises add a few drops of essence to flavor, then take off and soak in it slices of bread, cut with a paste-cutter and about half an inch thick. When well soaked, drain; dip them in beaten egg, roll in bread-crumbs, and fry and serve as fritters.

Glazed Fruit—Oranges glazed.—Oranges or any other fruit glazed, when mounted in a pyramid, is called *croque en bouche*.

Peel the oranges; then divide the carpels and free them from the pith, and put them away in a warm place for a few hours; they may be left over night. Cut very fine wire in pieces about eight inches long, bend each piece at both ends, forming a hook; then run one end or hook through the carpel of orange, and hang it on a stick placed on something horizontally. In order not to spill any of the juice, hook the orange near the edge of that part that was the centre of the orange before being divided, and as the other end of the wire forms a hook also, it is easy to hang it.

Prepare syrup of sugar, and when at the sixth degree take it from the fire, dip each carpel of orange into it and hang it again, and so on for the whole. As soon as dry enough to handle them, which takes hardly half a minute, pull off the wire and serve when perfectly cold.

To mount them in pyramid is not difficult, but requires time. When they are cold, prepare again the same syrup of sugar as above, and take it from the fire. While the sugar is on the fire take a tin mould, a plain one, larger at the top than at the bottom, and slightly grease it with sweet-oil. A convenient size for a family is, seven inches high, six inches broad at the top, and only four inches at the bottom.

Place one carpel of orange, resting on the bottom of the mould, along the side and the edge upward; as soon as the sugar is out of the fire, dip one of the two ends of another carpel into it, the edge only, and immediately place it as the first one, and touching it. The syrup being hot and liquid, the two pieces will adhere; do the same with others till you have one row around the bottom. Commence a second row as you did the first, but this time the first carpel you place must be dipped in sugar, in order to adhere to the first row, and all the others must also be dipped so as to adhere not only to the first piece placed, but also to the first row; and so on for each row till the mould is full, or till you have as much as you wish. As soon as cold, place a dish on the mould, turn upside down, and remove the mould. You have then a sightly dish, but not better than when served only glazed.

Another way to make it.—Grease with oil your marble for pastry, place the same mould as above over it but upside down, that is, the broader end down; grease the outside also with oil. Then place the rows of carpels of oranges all around outside of it, and in the same way as described above. The *croque en bouche* is more easily made this last way, but it is more difficult to remove the mould. Mould and fruit must be turned upside down carefully, after which the mould is pulled off.

If the syrup gets cold, it hardens, and cannot be used; in that state, add a little water and put it back on the fire, but it is difficult to rewarm it; generally it colors and is unfit. When that happens, make burnt sugar with it, or a *nougat.* It is better and safer to make a little of it, just what can be used before it gets cold, and if not enough, make some a second and even a third time. While the sugar is hot, and while you are dipping the fruit in it, be careful not to touch it, as it burns badly. In glazing the fruit first, some syrup falls in taking it from the pan to the stick; place your marble board, greased with oil, under, so that you can pick it without any trouble and use it.

Chestnuts, glazed.—Roast the chestnuts, skin them well, then hook, dip, and hook again on the stick as directed for pieces of oranges. A pyramid also may be made, and a sightly one it makes.

Cherries.—They must be picked with their stems, and by which you tie two together with a piece of twine. See that they are clean and dry, and have two sticks instead of one, placed parallel, about two inches apart, in order to prevent the two cherries from touching, when hung, as they would immediately adhere. Proceed for the rest as described for oranges.

Pears.—Small, ripe pears are excellent glazed; peel them, but leave the stem on, and then proceed as with cherries in every particular.

Strawberries or any other Berries.—The berries must be picked with the stem. Wash them in cold water, drain, dry, or wipe carefully, and then proceed as for cherries in every particular. A more delicate dish than strawberries or raspberries glazed cannot be made.

Grapes.—When clean, proceed as described for cherries.

Plums.—Take plums, well ripened and with the stems on, and proceed as with cherries.

Prunes.—Soak the prunes in tepid water, and when dry, hook them like carpels of orange, and finish in the same manner.

Currants.—When clean and dry, tie two clusters together, and proceed as for cherries.

Pine-Apple.—Cut pine-apple in dice, and proceed as described for carpels of orange.

Iced Fruit.—As a general rule, the more watery the fruit the more reduced the syrup of sugar must be. If it is not reduced enough, small pieces of ice, formed by the water of the fruit, will be found while eating it. The fruit must be ripe. It is done also with preserved fruit. It is impossible to tell exactly the degree or state of the fruit and syrup without a hydrometer.

The following *preparation* may be added to the fruit, or to *punch*, as soon as it begins to freeze; it is not indispensable, but gives it more body: Put one pound of loaf-sugar in a copper pan with two gills of cold water, set on the fire, stir now and then till it comes to a boil, then boil till it is at the fifth state or 43°, and take off. Beat four whites of eggs to a stiff froth, flavor with essence of vanilla, and turn the sugar into the eggs, little by little, but do not stop beating until the whole is in. Then move the mixture gently round with a spoon for about a minute, and it is ready for use.

With Peaches, Apricots, or Plums.—The following proportions are for one pint of juice. Peel and stone the fruit carefully, then mash it through a sieve into a bowl. Make one pint of syrup of sugar at 32°, and when cold turn it into the bowl and mix it with the pint of juice, add the juice of a rather large orange and a little of the rind grated, mix again, freeze as directed for ice-cream, and serve.

With Currants, Lemons, Oranges, Pears, Pine-Apples, Strawberries, and other Berries.—Proceed as for peaches in every particular, except that you press the juice of the currants and berries through a towel instead of mashing them through a sieve, and that you use the syrup at 44° for them also; the others are peeled and cored or seeded.

With Melons.—Proceed as for peaches, except that you add to the mixture a little *kirschwasser.*

With Preserved Fruit.—Use the syrup at 30°, and proceed as for peaches in every other particular.

Iced Coffee.—Make strong coffee, and when cold mix it with the same volume of thick cream, sweeten to taste, freeze, and serve.

Iced Chocolate.—Break in pieces about four ounces of chocolate, and set it on a slow fire in a tin pan, with two tablespoonfuls of water; when melted take it from the fire, add a gill of warm water, and work it with a spoon for five minutes; then mix it with the same volume of syrup of sugar at 30°, freeze and serve. The syrup is used when cold.

Iced Tea is made as iced coffee.

Sweet Jellies—Wine Jelly.—Soak two ounces of gelatin in a gill of cold water for about half an hour. Put in a block-tin saucepan three eggs and shells, three ounces of sugar, one quart of cold water; beat a little with an egg-beater to break the eggs, and mix the whole together; add also a few drops of burnt sugar, same of essence, rum, according to taste, from half a gill to half a pint, then the gelatin and water in which it is; set on a good fire, stirring slowly with an egg-beater, and stopping once in a while to see if it comes to a boil, when, stop stirring, keep boiling very slowly for two or three minutes, and turn into the jelly-bag, which you do as soon as clear; the process requires from two to three minutes. While it is boiling take a few drops with a spoon, and you will easily see when it is clear. Pass it through the bag three or four times, turn into a mould, put on ice, and when firm, put a dish on it, turn upside down, remove the mould, and serve.

Jelly Macédoine.—Make the same jelly as above, and pass it through the bag also; put some in a mould, say a thickness of half an inch, have the mould on ice; then, as soon as it is firm, place some fruit on that layer and according to fancy; and, with a tin ladle, pour more jelly into the mould, but carefully and slowly, in order not to upset the fruit you have in; continue pouring till you have a thickness of about half an inch on the fruit. Repeat this as many times as you please, and till the mould is full; vary the fruit at each layer, and especially the color of the different kinds. The color of the jelly may also be changed at every layer, by mixing in it more burnt sugar, some carmine or cochineal, some green spinach, a little in one layer and more in another. Any kind of ripe fruit can be used: strawberries, raspberries, stoned cherries, grapes, apples cut in fancy shapes; also peaches, bananas, etc.

Cold Wine-Jelly.—Put two ounces of gelatin in a bowl with a piece of cinnamon and a pint of cold water, and let stand about an hour. Then pour over about a quart of boiling water, and let stand about four minutes. After that, add two pounds of sugar, the juice of three lemons, a pint of sherry wine, and half a gill of brandy. Stir to dissolve the sugar, and turn the mixture into a mould through a strainer; place on ice, and serve as the above jellies.

Soufflés.—Put in a bowl four tablespoonfuls of potato-starch with three yolks of eggs, one ounce of butter, and a few drops of essence to flavor. Turn into it, little by little, stirring the while, about three gills of milk; set on the fire, stir continually, and take off at the first boiling. Stir continually but slowly. As soon as cold, beat three yolks of eggs with a tablespoonful of cold water, and mix them with the rest. Beat four whites of eggs to a stiff froth, and mix them also gently and slowly. Butter a mould well, fill it about two-thirds full, and bake in a warm but not quick oven (about 300° Fahr.). Besides being flavored with essence, *soufflés* may be flavored with coffee, lemon, orange, etc., according to taste. Generally, *soufflés* are served under the name of the object used to flavor them, such as *soufflé au café* (*soufflé* flavored with strong coffee), etc. They are all made in the same way as the above one, with the exception that they are flavored with strong coffee as above, and used instead of essence, or strong tea, chocolate, etc., or with a little jelly of different fruit, or with roasted chestnuts well pounded, instead of potato-starch, etc.

A hundred different kinds of *soufflés* can be easily made by following the above directions.

Apples, fried.—Peel and cut in small dice, dropping them in cold water till the whole is ready. Then fry with a little butter till about half cooked, when add a little water and sugar to taste; finish the cooking, take from the fire;

beat a yolk of egg with a teaspoonful of cold water and mix it with the apples; serve warm. Proceed in the same way with *pears*.

Peaches baked.—Cut peaches in two, remove the stone, and with a paste-cutter cut some slices of bread, and place them in a buttered bakepan with half of a peach on each, the skin downward; dust well with sugar, put a piece of butter the size of a kidney-bean on each, place in a rather slow oven; dish when cooked, turn the juice over, if any; if none, a little syrup of pears, and serve warm.

Do the same with *apricots*, *plums*, and slices of *pine-apples*. The slices of pine-apples may be soaked in *kirschwasser* for twenty-four hours before using them.

Prunes, stewed.—Wash them in cold water if necessary. Soak them in tepid water for about two hours, and set the whole on the fire; boil gently till half done, when add sugar to taste, a gill of claret wine to half a pound of prunes, and serve either warm or cold when done. If the water boils away too much, add more.

Currants, Blackberries, or other Fruit, for Dessert.—Beat well the white of an egg with a little water; dip the fruit in, and roll it immediately in some fine-crushed sugar; place it on a dish, and leave it thus five or six hours, and serve.

A more sightly and exquisite plate of dessert than a plate of currants dressed thus, cannot be had.

Besides all our receipts, any kind of fruit may be served for dessert, according to the season; also any kind of cheese; also fruits preserved in liquor.

Berries with Milk or Cream.—Nearly every kind of berries, when clean, may be served with milk or cream, and sugar to taste.

With Liquor.—They may also be served with brandy, rum, *kirschwasser*, whiskey, etc., and sugar.

Marmalades, or Preserves of Fruits—Of Apricots or Peaches.—Boil two pounds of peaches for a minute, take off and drop them immediately in cold water. Drain and skin immediately, cut in two and remove the stone. Crack two-thirds of the stones and throw the kernels in boiling water; leave them in till the skin comes off easily; skin them well and cut them in small pieces, lengthwise. Lay the peaches in a pan, with about a pound and a half of sugar, set on the fire, boil about twenty minutes, stirring the while with a wooden spoon; a few minutes before taking from the fire, put also the kernels in the pan; then turn in pots or jars as soon as off the fire. Cover well when cold, and keep in a dry and cool (but not cold) closet.

Of Plums.—Proceed as for the above.

Of Pears and Quinces.—Quarter, peel, and core the fruit, put it in a pan, and proceed for the rest as directed for peaches, except that you use sweet almonds instead of kernels.

Of Blackberries, Cherries, Currants, Raspberries, and other like Berries.— Wash the fruit in cold water, drain, dry, and mash it through a sieve placed over a saucepan; when the juice and pulp are in the pan add the same weight of loaf-sugar as that of juice, which is easily ascertained by weighing the pan first; set on the fire, skim it carefully; it takes about half an hour to cook; then put in pots and let cool; cut a piece of white paper the size of the inside of the pot, dip it in brandy, put it over the fruit, cover the pots, and place them in a dry and cool closet.

Of Grapes.—Select well-ripened grapes and pick the berries. Put them in a thick towel, and press the juice out, which you put in a copper or brass saucepan, set on a good fire, and boil till about half reduced. Skim off the scum, and stir now and then while it is on the fire. Then add about half a pound of loaf-sugar to a pound of juice, boil again fifteen or twenty minutes, take off, put in pots or jars, cover or cork well when cold, and put away in a dark and cool closet.

Candied or Comfited Fruit.—The best state of the fruit to be candied is just when commencing to ripen or a little before. It must be picked in dry weather, and be sound; the least stain is enough to spoil it soon after it is preserved.

Peaches.—Make a cut on the side of the fruit and remove the stone without bruising it; then skin it carefully and drop it in a pan of cold water. When they are all in, set on the fire, boil gently till they float. There must be much more water than is necessary to cover them, in order to see easily when they come to the surface. Then take them off carefully, with a skimmer, and drop them in cold water and drain. When drained, put them in a pan, cover them with syrup of sugar after it is skimmed and clarified. (*See* Syrup of Sugar.) The syrup must be boiling when turned over the fruit. Set on the fire, give one boil only, and turn the whole into a bowl, which you cover with paper, and leave thus twelve or fifteen hours. After that time, drain, put the syrup on the fire, the peaches in the bowl, and at the first boiling of the syrup, turn it over the fruit, cover the bowl with paper, and leave about as long, that is, twelve or fifteen hours.

Repeat the same process three times more, in all five times. The last time the syrup must be at the first state as described for syrup of sugar. Inexperienced persons will do well to try at first with a few fruits, and go through the whole process, after which it will be comparatively easy.

Every one is awkward in doing a thing for the first time, and does not do it well, however easy or simple it may be. That is the reason why societies of farmers make better preserves than other people; they teach one another; and besides, no one is allowed to touch the fruit before having seen it done several times.

Candied fruit, as well as preserves, get spoiled by fermentation, if not cooked enough; by moisture, if kept in a damp place; or by heat, if kept in a warm place.

When the last process has been gone through, leave the fruit in the bowl about twenty-four hours; then put it in jars, cover air-tight, and put away in a dry and cool closet. It may also be drained, dried on a riddle in a warm place, and kept in boxes. A wooden riddle or screen is better than a metal one. They may also be put in decanters, covered with brandy or other liquor, and corked well. When preserved in brandy, it is not necessary to remove the stone; they may be covered with half syrup and half brandy.

Plums.—Pick them just before commencing to ripen, and cut the stem half way. When clean, but neither stoned nor skinned, prick them around the stem with a fork, drop them in cold water, set on the fire, add a gill of vinegar to three quarts of water, and take from the fire as soon as they float.

Drain, put them in a bowl, pour boiling syrup of sugar over them, and proceed as directed for peaches, that is, cover and pour the syrup on them five times in all. They are kept like peaches also, either in jars, dried, or in brandy.

Pears.—After being peeled and the stem cut off half way, they may be preserved whole or in quarters. In peeling them, they must be dropped in cold water with a little lemon-juice to keep them white. They are picked just before commencing to ripen. When ready, put cold water and the juice of a lemon to every two quarts in a deep pan, and drop the pears in, set on the fire and boil gently till well done; take off, drain and drop in cold water, which you change two or three times and without stopping; then drain again, place them in a large bowl, and then proceed as for peaches. They are kept like peaches also.

Apples.—Proceed as for pears, except that apples are cooked much quicker.

Pine-Apples.—Peel, slice, and drop the fruit in cold water; add a little sugar, set on the fire and boil gently till done, when drain and drop in cold water and drain again. Put them in a bowl, and proceed as for peaches for the rest, with the exception that they are kept in jars only, and not dried or put in brandy.

Chestnuts.—Skin the chestnuts and put them in cold water on the fire, and take off when tender; then remove the under skin or white envelope or pith. Place them in a bowl, and proceed as for peaches for the rest.

Oranges.—Drop oranges in boiling water and take off when the rind is tender, and when a darning-needle can be run through it easily. Drain and drop them in cold water. After two or three hours drain, cut in slices, and put them in a bowl; then proceed as for peaches, except that they are kept in jars only.

Quinces.—Peel, quarter, and core quinces just before they commence ripening, drop in boiling water; drain them when done, and drop them immediately in cold water. As soon as cold, take them off, drain and put them in a bowl. For the rest, proceed as for peaches, with the exception that they are only kept in jars, but neither dried nor put in brandy.

To Preserve in Brandy.—Besides the dried fruits above described, several may be preserved in brandy, without being cooked and soaked in syrup of sugar.

Cherries.—Pick them when fully ripe, see that they are clean, and put them in decanters with cloves, pieces of cinnamon, and entirely covered with brandy; cover well, but do not cork, and leave thus two weeks, at the end of which, place a colander over a vessel and empty the decanters into it; pass the liquor through a jelly-bag, mix it with some syrup of sugar at the second degree, turn over the fruit which you cover with it, and cork the decanters well when perfectly cold. Keep in a dark, cool, and dry place.

Do the same with strawberries and other like fruit.

Fruit Jellies—With Apples or Quinces.—Peel, core, and cut in small pieces two quarts of good apples or quinces, lay them in a stewpan with a clove well pounded, and the juice of half a lemon; cover with water, set on a moderate fire, and boil slowly till well cooked. Turn into a jelly-bag, or a thick towel under which you place a vessel to receive the juice, and when it is all out, put it in a stewpan with three-quarters of a pound of sugar to every pound of juice; boil to a jelly.

As soon as done put it in pots or jars, let cool, cut a piece of white paper the size of the inside of the pot, dip it in brandy, put it over the jelly, cover the pot well, and place in a dry, cool closet, but not too cold. What remains in the bag may be used to make a *compote*. Watch the process carefully, skimmer in hand, to skim off the scum, and stir now and then, lest it should burn.

With Apricots, Peaches, Plums, etc.—After having taken the stones out, cut them in four pieces, and proceed as for apple-jelly above in every other particular.

With Blackberries, Currants, Grapes, Raspberries, or other like Berries.—Put the well-ripened berries in a coarse towel and squeeze all the juice out of them, which you put into a stewpan with as many pounds of loaf-sugar as there are of juice, and finish as directed for apple-jelly. A little rum or essence of rose, or any other, according to taste, may be added just before taking from the fire.

Punch.—Put a saltspoonful of black tea in a crockery pot, with one clove, a little cinnamon, and the rind of a lemon cut in pieces; pour on the whole half a pint of boiling water; let it remain thus five minutes, and strain. Put a bottle of rum or brandy in a crockery vessel, with twelve ounces of loaf-sugar, set the rum or brandy on fire, and let burn till it stops. Then mix tea and rum together, and it is ready for use. It is drunk cold or warm, according to taste. When wanted warm, if made previously, set it on a moderate fire, in a tin or crockery kettle.

It keeps very well if carefully bottled and corked when cold.

Another way to make it is to mix the rum or brandy with the tea without burning it. It is warmed, used, and kept like the above. The quantity of water may be reduced or augmented, according to taste, and so also the sugar.

Another.—Grate the rind of a lemon and of two oranges on a piece of sugar, the yellow part only, and put it in a bowl with cold water to dissolve it; then add two gills of pine-apple syrup, essence of vanilla, a pint of claret wine, a pint of Catawba, Sauterne, or Rhine wine, a pint of Champagne, and a gill of brandy; sweeten to taste; strain, put on ice for some time, and serve.

Another.—Put a pound of sugar in a bowl with a gill of water to dissolve it; then add the juice of three oranges, a little rind grated, a bottle of Champagne and one of Catawba or Sauterne wine; strain, place on ice for some time, and serve cold.

Roman Punch.—Make iced lemon with one quart of juice, same of syrup as directed, then mix with it the juice of four oranges, some lemon and orange rind grated, and about three gills of rum (or according to taste); also, if liked, the preparation used for iced fruit. Then put the mixture in the freezer, stir while freezing, and serve. It must not be frozen hard, as it is better when served rather liquid and frothy. It may be made with any other liquor, if preferred.

Punch is served either after the *entrées* or after the *relevés* of fish, according to taste.

PASTRY.

Of all the branches of the science and art of cooking, pastry, if not the most difficult, requires the greatest care. An inferior piece of meat makes an inferior dish, but still it can be eaten without danger: but inferior pastry can hardly be eaten; or, if eaten, it is indigestible. We will recommend our readers to be very careful about proportions; it would not make a great difference for some kinds, but for others, putting too much or too little of one or more things would certainly result in failure. It is very important to have good materials. New flour is very inferior for pastry; it must have been ground for at least three months. Always keep it in bags, and in a dry and well-ventilated place. Sift before using it. Use fresh eggs, good butter, and good pulverized sugar.

The most important of all is the oven, for, supposing that you have used good materials, have mixed them well, if not properly baked, every thing is lost, materials and labor. Supposing that you have a good oven, there is still a difficulty—and if the last, not the least—the degree of heat. Some require a quick oven, as puff-paste, *choux*, etc.; others a warm one, and others a slow oven, as *meringues* biscuits, etc. By putting the hand in the oven you can tell if it is properly heated, but it requires experience, and even practitioners are often mistaken; therefore, the easiest way is to have a thermometer in the oven. It may be placed in the oven of every stove or range; it is only necessary to bore a hole on the top of the range or stove, reaching the oven, and have a thermometer with the bulb inclosed in a brass sheath, perforated, long enough to reach the oven, and of the size of the hole bored—the glass tube being above the top of the range.

Pastes.—There are several kinds of paste. Puff-paste is the most important; it can be made very rich, rich, and less so; and several hundred different cakes can be made with it. Small cakes are called *petits fours*.

The next in importance is the *pâte-à-choux*; then the paste for meat-pies, sometimes called *pâte brisée*.

Puff-paste requires care, but is easily made; *pâte-à-choux* must be well worked.

Puff-paste.—To make good puff-paste, good flour and butter, free from salt or sour milk, are indispensable. It must be made in a cool place. Take half a pound of good butter and knead it well in a bowl of cold water; if fresh and not salt, the kneading will take the sour milk out of it; if salty, it will remove the salt, then put it in another bowl of cold water and leave it till it is perfectly firm, and then use. When the butter is ready, put half a pound of flour on the paste-board or marble, make a hole in it, in which you put a pinch of salt, and cold water enough to make a rather stiff dough. It requires about half a pint of water, knead well, make a kind of ball with the dough, and put it on a corner of your marble or paste-board. Take the butter from the water and knead it on the board, to press all the water out of it. Give it the shape of a large sausage; dredge the board slightly with flour, roll the butter over only once, as it must take very little of it, dredge both ends of the piece of butter with flour also, then by putting one end on the board and pressing on the other end with your hands, you will flatten it of a rather round shape, and till of about half an inch in thickness. Put it thus on the corner of the board also. Immediately after having prepared the butter, take the dough and roll it down, of a round form also, and till large enough to envelop the butter in it easily. Remember that during the whole operation of folding and rolling the paste down, you must dust the marble or paste-board with flour, very slightly and often; do the same on the top of the paste. It is done in order to prevent the paste from adhering to the board or to the rolling-pin. It must be dusted slightly, so that the paste cannot absorb much of it, as it would make it tough. Have a slab of marble or slate; it is much easier than wood, and cooler.

When the dough is spread, place the butter right on the middle of it. Turn one side of the dough over the butter, covering it a little more than half way; do the game with the opposite side, the dough lapping over that of the first side turned; do the same with the side toward you, and also with the side opposite. Dough stretching easily when pulled, and contracting easily when let loose after having pulled it, you have now still four corners of the dough to bring over the butter and in the same way as above, and by doing which, you give to the whole a somewhat round form, and also have the butter perfectly enveloped in the dough. Place the rolling-pin on the middle of the paste, horizontally, and press gently on it so as to make a furrow; do the same from place to place, on the whole surface, making furrows about an inch apart. Repeat the process again, this time placing the rolling-pin right on the top of each elevated line; and again, repeat it a third time, also placing the pin on each elevated line. Now do exactly the same contrariwise. Then, roll the paste down, gently, evenly, to a thickness of about one fourth of an inch, and of a rectangular shape. Fold it in three by turning over one-third of its length toward the other end, and thus covering another third of it; fold or turn over the remaining third, so as to cover the first third turned over. Roll it down again of about the same thickness as above, but without making furrows in it; give it also the same rectangular shape, taking care to make the length of what was the width, *i. e.* extending it the longer way in an opposite direction to that of the first time, so that the ends will be what the sides were. Fold in three as before, put it on a plate and set in a refrigerator for from ten to twenty minutes. Take hold of it again, roll down as above, fold in the same way also, and put away for ten minutes. You roll down and fold from four to six times, not counting the time you envelop the butter in the dough. In cold weather, and when the butter is firm, fold and roll only four times; but in rather warm weather, fold and roll six times. If it is too warm, it is of no use to try with butter.

Puff-paste may be made without stopping; that is, without putting it away in a cool place for some time; but it is better to let it rest; it is lighter and rises better. When finished, it can be used immediately; but it is better also to put it in a plate or dish, cover it with a towel, and put it in a refrigerator for from twelve to twenty-four hours. Although it must be kept in a cool place, do not put it near enough to the ice to freeze. It may be kept thus for two or three days.

Puff-paste with Beef-Suet.—Take half a pound of fresh beef suet, the nearest the kidney the best; break it in small pieces with the hands, at the same time removing the thin skin and fibres as much as possible; put it in a bowl of cold water and knead well till it is rather soft; take it off, mash and bruise it well on the paste-board with a rolling-pin; knead it again like butter; roll it in flour like butter also, and proceed as above for the rest, and with the same proportion, weight for weight of flour and beef-suet, but it requires more salt. Beef-suet being more firm than butter, puff-paste can be made with it during summer, but it must be eaten immediately, being very inferior after a while.

The proportion of butter and flour may be varied. Weight for weight makes the real puff-paste, and very rich. If less butter is used it will not rise as much, but is excellent nevertheless, and is more handy to make different cakes, such as short-cakes with fruit. Therefore puff-paste may be made with the following proportions: to one pound of flour, use fourteen, twelve, ten, eight, or even four ounces of butter or suet. Another way is to mix one or two eggs in the flour, water, and salt before rolling it down. When eggs are used, it requires less water. Envelop the butter in it in the same way.

Allumettes.—Cut strips of puff-paste of any length, about three inches wide and about one-fifth of an inch in thickness; mix well together, and for about three or four minutes, one ounce of sugar and about half the white of an egg; spread this mixture over the strips of paste, so as to have a rather thin coat of it; then cut the paste across, so as to make small strips about one inch broad and three inches long. Bake in an oven at about 400 deg. Fahr.

Feuillettés.—Roll puff-paste down to a thickness of from one-eighth to one-half of an inch in thickness; cut it in pieces of any size and shape, according to fancy with a knife or with a paste-cutter; glaze the top only with egg, and bake in an oven at about 450 deg. Fahr.

Feuillettés à la Condé.—Roll and cut the paste exactly as for the above; then, instead of baking it, fry it in hot fat (*see* FRYING); turn into a colander when fried, dust with sugar, and serve as warm as possible.

Pommées.—Line the bottom of a bakepan with puff-paste, about one-eighth of an inch in thickness; spread stewed apples over it of a thickness of one-quarter of an inch; cover these with another thickness of puff-paste; prick the cover all over with the point of a knife, and bake in an oven at about 400 deg. Fahr. When baked, cut it in square pieces, dust with sugar, and serve hot or cold, according to taste.

Porte-manteaux.—Cut strips of puff-paste of any length, about three inches broad, and one-eighth of an inch in thickness; spread on the middle of the strips, and lengthwise, some frangipane, or stewed apples, or any kind of sweetmeats, of the size of the finger. Then turn one side of the paste over the frangipane or sweetmeats, glaze the border with egg (we mean by "the border," about half an inch in width, measuring from the edge); then turn the other side over it so that the glazing will cause the two pastes to stick together. Thus it will be only a little over an inch broad and about half an inch thick. Cut the strips across in small pieces about two inches long, glaze the top with egg, and then bake in an oven at 400 deg. Fahr.

Tartelettes.—Roll some puff-paste down to a thickness of about one-sixteenth of an inch; cut it, with a paste-cutter, of the size of small tin moulds, and place the pieces in the moulds; put about a teaspoonful of frangipane in each; place two narrow strips of paste across each, which strips you cut with a truckle; bake in an oven at about 380 deg. Fahr.

Tartelettes (sweet).—Proceed as for the above in every particular, except that you use any kind of sweetmeats or jelly instead of frangipane.

Cake Pithiviers.—Roll some puff-paste down to a thickness of about one-eighth of an inch; cut it round and place on a baking-pan; if the pan be square or rectangular, cut a round piece that will go in easily; cut a strip of paste about one inch broad, glaze with egg the border of the paste in the pan, place the strip all around, and then glaze it also. Fill the middle with the following mixture: pound four ounces of sweet almonds and mix them well with half a pound of sugar, two ounces of butter, four yolks of eggs, essence to flavor, and four macaroons chopped. Cut another piece of puff-paste round, and of the same size as the other; dust it slightly with flour, fold it gently in four; the piece then will have two straight sides and a circular one. With a sharp knife make three cuts in each of the two straight sides through the four thicknesses of the paste, and about half an inch in length. Make another cut through the paste also, representing half of the figure 8, right in the middle of the piece of paste, commencing half an inch from the border of the circular side and in the middle of it, and going toward the point, so that when the paste is open there are sixteen cuts in it. Place the paste still folded on the paste and mixture in the pan, the circular side on the border and the point right in the middle; open it gently, and the whole will be covered. Glaze with egg, and put in an oven at from 430 to 460 deg. Fahr. The same cake may be filled with a frangipane, and prepared as the above for the rest.

Rissoles (also called Fourrés).—Cut round pieces of puff-paste about three inches in diameter; wet the edge with water, put a teaspoonful of compote or any kind of sweetmeat on one side of it, then fold the paste in two, so as to cover the sweetmeat; pinch the paste around to cause it to adhere, in order to envelop the sweetmeat; you have then a cake of a semicircular shape. Glaze with egg, bake in a quick oven, dust with sugar, and serve.

Galette du Gymnase.—Make puff-paste with half a pound of butter to a pound of flour, and when done as directed, knead it. Then roll it down to the thickness of about one-fourth of an inch, cut it in strips of any length and about an inch and a half wide, glaze with egg, bake in a quick oven, about 420 deg. Fahr. The two ends of the strips may be brought together and joined, forming a crown. The same *galette* is made with trimmings of puff-paste, kneaded and rolled as above.

Fanchonnettes.—These are made with the same puff-paste as the *galette* above; then cut it in round pieces, place them on small moulds, fill them with any kind of sweetmeats and frangipane, with almonds, half of each; bake, dust with sugar, and serve. Instead of frangipane, spread raisins over the sweetmeats, or almonds, peanuts, hazel-nuts, etc., all cut in small strips, lengthwise; you make then an infinite number of different small cakes.

Fans.—Make some puff-paste with equal weight of flour and butter, fold and roll it down six times, and put in a cold place. Leave it of a thickness of about one-quarter of an inch; cut it with a sharp knife in pieces of a rectangular shape, about four inches long and two broad, which cut again in two, across and from one corner to the other, so that you make two pieces of a right-angled triangle shape. Place the pieces on their sides in a bake-pan, on their sides, far apart, and bake in a very quick oven. When done, dust with sugar, and serve.

Vol-au-vent and *bouchées* for the day's use are baked early in the morning. They are warmed in a slow oven just before filling them.

Vol-au-vent.—A *vol-au-vent* is made with puff-paste and filled with oysters, meat, etc., when baked; that is, when the cake is baked and emptied, it is warmed in the oven, filled, and served warm. It is made of an oval or round shape. When made small it is generally of a round shape, but when made rather large it is generally of an oval shape. When the puff-paste is ready to be used, roll down to any thickness from one-quarter to three-quarters of an inch; cut it with a sharp-pointed knife of the size and shape you wish, then with the same knife cut what is called the cover, *i. e.*, make a cut all around, about half an inch from the edge or border, and about one-third through the paste, leaving two-thirds of the thickness of the paste uncut. This operation is called marking out the cover. Glaze the top of the paste with egg, and bake it in a very quick oven, about 500 deg. Fahr. In glazing, be careful not to glaze the sides or allow any egg to run on the sides; it would prevent the paste from rising. Some drawings may be made on the cover with the back of a knife, according to fancy: leaves, for instance, are very easily imitated; it is only necessary to run the knife on the paste, without cutting it. When in the oven, do not look at it for at least seven or eight minutes, for in opening the door of the oven it might cause the paste to fall and even after that time open and shut the door quickly; take off when properly baked. When the oven is hot enough it takes about twelve minutes, and even less time when the *vol-au-vent* is small. Take from the oven when baked, and immediately run the point of the knife all around and in the same place as you did before being baked, which place is well marked. Thus you cut off the cover and remove it, then remove also all the unbaked paste that is inside of the *vol-au-vent*, so that you have left what may be called a shell. Keep it then till the oysters or meat are ready to put in it. About five minutes before the filling is ready, put the shell or baked paste in a slow oven to warm it, turn the filling into it, enough to fill it entirely; place the cover on the top, and serve warm. The unbaked paste removed from the inside is baked, and makes an excellent cake, though not a sightly one.

Another.—Cut a piece of puff-paste the same as for the above one, that is, either round or oval, and of the size you wish. Instead of marking a cover, glaze the border with egg. It is understood here by "the border," a space about three-quarters of an inch broad and all around it, the space being measured from the edge toward the centre. Then cut a strip of puff-paste about three-quarters of an inch broad, long enough to cover the place or space glazed, which strip you put all around the first paste, and you then have a border. The place between the two pastes being glazed, they will adhere in baking. Then also glaze the upper side of the border carefully with egg. With a knife or fork, prick the paste, inside of the border only, in ten, fifteen, or twenty places, according to the size of the *vol-au-vent*, and in order to prevent that part from rising as much as it would if not pricked. Bake in the same oven as the above—a very quick one.

A *vol-au-vent* thus made is deeper than the first one, having two thicknesses of paste. Generally there is little or no paste (unbaked) to remove; having pricked the centre, it prevents it from rising and bakes it evenly, but if there is any, remove it. A cover may be made by cutting a piece of puff-paste of the size of the *vol-au-vent* and baking it separately. It may be decorated with the back of the knife as the above one, and made convex on the top by baking it on a piece of tin. It is warmed, filled, and served the same as the above.

A *vol-au-vent* is filled with the following:

With Oysters.—The quantity is according to the size of the *vol-au-vent*. Blanch one quart of oysters. Put two ounces of butter in a saucepan, set it on the fire, and when melted add a tablespoonful of flour; stir, and when turning rather yellow add also about a pint of milk, and the liquor from the oysters; stir, and as soon as it turns rather thick put the oysters in, taking care to have them free from pieces of the shell. Give one boil, add salt to taste, two yolks of eggs, stir again, turn into the warm paste, place the cover on, and serve warm.

With Lobster.—Prepare the lobster as for *bouchées*, fill the shell with it, and serve warm.

With Cod-fish.—Prepare fresh cod-fish *à la Béchamel*, fill the *vol-au-vent* or shell with it, and serve warm.

With Turbot.—Proceed as for cod-fish in every particular.

With Eels.—Fill the *vol-au-vent* with eels, oyster sauce, or in *poulette*, and serve warm.

With Chicken.—Fill with a chicken or part of a chicken in *fricassée* or *sauté*.

With Livers and Combs of Chicken.—Prepare combs and livers of chicken in *fricassée*, the same as a chicken, fill the *vol-au-vent* with them. Serve hot.

With Sweetbreads.—Cook the sweetbreads as directed, and fill the *vol-au-vent* with them. Serve warm.

With Veal.—Fill the *vol-au-vent* with veal in *blanquette*, in *ragout*, or in *bourgeoise*, and serve. It is generally filled with what has been left the day previous, as it requires very little for a *vol-au-vent*.

With Brains.—It may be filled with brains of calf, pig, sheep, or veal; prepared in *poulette*, or stewed.

With Rabbit.—Fill it with part of a rabbit *sauté*.

It may also be filled with any other *meat* or *fish*, according to taste, and being cooked previously.

With Fruits.—Fill the *vol-au-vent* with any kind of stewed fruit, jelly, sweetmeats, etc. It may be only filled, or the fruit may be dressed in pyramid inside of it.

Bouchées.—Bouchées, or *petites bouchées*, as they are sometimes called, are small, round *vol-au-vent*, served warm. They are also called *bouchées de dames* and *petites bouchées*. Roll puff-paste down to a thickness of about one-quarter of an inch, cut it with a paste-cutter of any size, mark the cover, and bake in an oven at about 450° Fahr. A good size is about three inches in diameter. When cut, take another paste-cutter about two inches in diameter, place it on the piece of paste; press on it just enough to mark the place where it was, but not enough to cut the paste, remove it and then the cover is marked; that is, you have a circle on the top of the paste, half an inch from the edge all around. Glaze with egg and bake. Make one for each person. Immediately on taking them from the oven, cut off the cover with a sharp-pointed knife. That is easily done; it is only necessary to follow the mark made with the paste-cutter, which is just as visible as before baking. Remove the cover and then carefully take out some unbaked paste inside of the *bouchée*, fill with lobster prepared as directed below, put the cover on, and serve as warm as possible.

The Filling.—Cut some flesh of boiled lobster in dice. Put two ounces of butter in a saucepan and set it on the fire; when melted, add a tablespoonful of flour, stir for about one minute, and add also broth (the quantity must be according to the number of *bouchées*, but we will give here the quantity necessary for five or six *bouchées*), about three gills, also salt, pepper, then the cut lobster; stir now and then for five or six minutes, and use.

Of Oysters.—Prepare, fill and serve exactly as the above, except that you fill with oysters prepared as for *vol-au-vent*, instead of filling with lobster.

Of Cod-fish.—Fill the *bouchées* with cod-fish, prepared *à la Béchamel*, and serve warm.

Of Eels.—Have some eels prepared either in *poulette* or oyster-sauce, fill the *bouchées*, and serve warm.

Of Turbot.—It is filled with turbot *à la crème* or *à la Béchamel*.

It may also be filled with any kind of fish, prepared *à la Béchamel, à la crème,* in white sauce, oyster-sauce, etc.

Of Truffles.—Cut the white flesh of a chicken in dice, prepare it as a chicken *sauté*, using truffles but no mushrooms, fill the *bouchées* with it and serve warm.

Of Purée of Chicken, or Bouchées de Dames.—It is filled with some *purée* of chicken, and served as warm as possible.

Do the same with a *purée* of game.

Of Bobolink.—Prepare and clean twelve bobolinks as directed for birds, put a teaspoonful of truffles, cut in small dice, in each bird, for stuffing; sew the incision, and bake or roast the birds. Put each bird in a *bouchée*, and serve warm. A more delicate dish cannot be made.

The same may be done with any kind of *small bird*.

Bouchées are generally served on a napkin and on a dish, in pyramid.

Pâte à choux.—Weigh four ounces of flour, to which add half a teaspoonful of sugar. Put two gills of cold water in a tin saucepan with two ounces of butter, and set it on the fire, stir a little with a wooden spoon to melt the butter before the water boils. At the first boiling of the water, throw into it the four ounces of flour and stir very fast with the spoon, holding the pan fast with the left hand. As soon as the whole is thoroughly mixed, take from the fire, but continue stirring for about fifteen or twenty seconds. It takes hardly half a minute from the time the flour is dropped in the pan to that when taken from the fire. The quicker it is done, the better. When properly done, nothing at all sticks to the pan, and by touching it with the finger it feels as soft as velvet, and does not adhere to it at all. Let it stand two or three minutes, then mix well with it, by means of a spoon, one egg; then another, and so on; in all four. It takes some time and work to mix the eggs, especially to mix the first one, the paste being rather stiff. They are added one at a time, in order to mix them better. If the eggs are small, add half of one or one more. To use only half a one, it is necessary to beat it first. Let the paste stand half an hour, stir again a little, and use. If it is left standing for some time and is found rather dry, add a little egg, which mix, and then use.

Beignets Soufflés—(also called *Pets de Nonne*).—Make some *pâte à choux*; take a small tablespoonful of it, holding the spoon with the left hand, and with the forefinger of the right cause the paste to fall in hot fat on the fire (*see* FRYING), turn over and over again till fried, then turn into a colander, dust with sugar, and serve hot. In frying, the paste will swell four or five times its size, and by dropping it carefully and as nearly of a round shape as possible, the cakes will be nearly round when done.

Choux or Cream Cakes.—Make some *pâte à choux*: have a buttered bakepan, and drop the paste upon it in the same way as you drop the *beignets* above; glaze with egg, and bake in an oven at about 380° Fahr. When baked and cold, make a cut on one side, about two-thirds through, the cut to be horizontal, a little above the middle, then, by raising the top a little, fill the cake, which is hollow, with one of the following creams: *whipped, Chantilly, cuite, frangipane,* or *légère*; dust with sugar, and serve.

The same, with Almonds.—Blanch sweet almonds and cut them in small strips, lengthwise; then, when the choux are in the bakepan and glazed with egg, spread the almonds all over, bake, fill, and serve as the above.

Saint Honoré.—Make some *pâte à choux.* Then put four tablespoonfuls of flour on the paste-board with two of sugar, one egg, one ounce of butter, salt, and a pinch of cinnamon; mix and knead the whole well; roll the paste down to a thickness of about one quarter of an inch and place it in a bakepan. Put a dessert-plate upside down on the paste, and cut it all around the plate with a knife; remove what is cut off and also the plate. Spread some *pâte à choux*, about a teaspoonful, all over the paste left in the bakepan, about one-sixteenth of an inch in thickness; put some of it also in the pastry-bag, and by squeezing it out, make a border with it about the size of the finger; prick the middle of the paste in about a dozen places with a fork and inside of the border; glaze the border with egg, and then bake in an oven at about 400° Fahr. While the above is baking, make very small *choux* (about the size of a macaroon), and bake them also. When both are baked, and while they are cooking, make some *crème légère*, fill the inside of the cake with it, so as to imitate a sugar-loaf or mound, about four inches in height, smooth it or scallop it with a knife. Put two tablespoonfuls of sugar and two of water in a saucepan, set it on the fire, toss the pan occasionally to boil evenly, and till it becomes like syrup. Do not stir too much, else it will turn white and somewhat like molasses-candy. It is reduced enough when, by dipping (not stirring) a little stick in it and dipping it again immediately in cold water, the syrup-like liquor that has adhered to it breaks easily and is very transparent. It must be as transparent as glass. As soon as reduced thus, take from the fire and use. Dip the top of each small *chou* in it, holding the *chou* with a small knife stuck in it; place a piece of candy (generally, sugar-plums of various colors are used) on the top of each *chou*; place them apart and around the *crème légère,* and upon the border of the cake, with one a little larger than the others on the top of it; serve cold. This cake is as good as it is sightly.

Eclairs.—Eclairs are also called *petits pains* or *profiterolles au chocolat*.

Eclairs au Chocolat.—Make some *pâte à choux* as directed above, and put it in the pastry-bag with tube No. 1 at the end of it. Force it out of the bag into a baking-pan greased with butter. By closing and holding up the larger end of the bag and by pressing it downward, it will come out of the tube in a rope-like shape and of the size of the tube. Draw the bag toward you while pressing, and stop when you have spread a length of about four inches. Repeat this operation till the baking-pan is full or till the paste is all out. Leave a space of about two inches between each cake, as they swell in baking. Bake in an oven at about 370 degrees. When baked and cold, slit one side about half through, open gently and fill each cake with the following cream, and then close it. Cream: put in a block-tin saucepan three tablespoonfuls of sugar, two of flour, four yolks of eggs, and mix well with a wooden spoon. Add a pint of milk, little by little, and mixing the while; set on the fire, stir continually till it becomes rather thick, and take off. Have one ounce of chocolate melted on a slow fire in half a gill of milk, and mix it with the rest, and use. Put one ounce of chocolate in a tin saucepan with a teaspoonful of water, and set on a slow fire; when melted, mix with it two tablespoonfuls of sugar, stir for a while; that is, till it is just thick enough to spread it over the cakes, and not liquid enough to run down the sides. A thickness of about one-sixteenth of an inch is sufficient. The cakes may either be dipped in the chocolate or the chocolate may be spread over them with a knife. Serve cold.

Eclairs au Café.—It is made exactly like the above, except that you mix with the cream three tablespoonfuls of strong coffee, instead of chocolate and milk.

Eclairs au Thé.—It is made like the preceding one, with the exception that strong tea is used instead of strong coffee.

Eclairs à la Vanille.—Proceed as for the above, but mix a teaspoonful of essence of vanilla in the cream instead of tea.

Eclairs à l'Essence.—The meaning of *éclairs à l'essence* is, that a few drops of any kind of essence are mixed with the cream instead of chocolate and milk, and prepared and served like the others.

Eclairs aux Fraises.—Instead of filling the cakes with cream, fill them with strawberry-jelly, and for the rest proceed as for *éclairs au chocolat*.

Eclairs aux Groseilles.—Made like the above, but filled with currant-jelly.

Do the same with *apple, blackberry, cherry, grape, peach, pear, plum, quince, raspberry jelly*, etc.

Petits Pains à la Reine.—*Eclairs* are so called when filled with marmalade of peaches in which sweet almonds chopped fine have been mixed previously.

Petits Pains à la Rose.—Like the above, and by adding a few drops of essence of roses to the marmalade.

Petits Pains à l'Essence.—Like the above, with any kind of essence: *pink, violet, geranium*, etc.

Biscuits in Boxes.—Make some square boxes with sheets of white paper; fill them about two-thirds full with the same mixture as for lady's fingers, dust with sugar, and bake in a slow oven; serve cold.

With Almonds.—Mix well together with a wooden spoon four yolks of eggs with four ounces of sugar (pulverized), add three ounces of flour and mix well again. Beat the four whites to a stiff froth, and then have somebody to turn the mixture into them while you finish beating, and then mix the whole gently but well. It must not be stirred too much. Have two ounces of bitter almonds well pounded, with a teaspoonful of sugar, and mix them with the rest. Butter small moulds, turn the mixture into them, filling about two-thirds full, glaze with egg, dust with sugar, and bake in an oven at about 300 degrees Fahr.; serve cold.

With Chocolate.—Make some biscuits like the above, omitting the almonds, and flavoring them with a few drops of essence of vanilla. When cold, glaze them with chocolate, the same as described for *éclairs*, and serve.

With Essence.—Make biscuits with almonds or without, as the above ones, and flavor them with any kind of essence, or with orange and lemon rind grated.

Glazed.—When the biscuits are baked, glaze them with icing, and serve cold. These are sometimes called *biscuits à la royale*.

Of Rheims.—Mix well in a bowl six yolks of eggs with six ounces of sugar, with a wooden spoon. Add and mix with the above five ounces of flour and lemon-rind grated; beat four whites of eggs to a stiff froth, and mix them also with the rest. Butter small moulds, turn the mixture into them, and bake in a slow oven, about 300 degrees Fahr. These are often made of the shape of lady's fingers. They are excellent eaten with wine.

With Filberts.—Put ten or twelve ounces of filberts or peanuts in a mortar with a few drops of orange-flower water and about half the white of an egg; when reduced to a paste, mix well with it four ounces of sifted flour, eight ounces of fine, white sugar, the yolks of two eggs well beaten, and the whites of four eggs whisked to a froth; when the whole is properly mixed, put it into a well-buttered mould, which place in a moderately-heated oven; watch it carefully, take out when cooked, which is easily known by the color it assumes.

Biscuits with hazel-nuts, peach, or other kernels, may be made in the same way; that is, using them instead of filberts.

Lady's Fingers.—Mix well together with a wooden spoon four yolks of eggs and four ounces of pulverized sugar, then add three ounces of flour and mix well again. Beat four whites of eggs to a stiff froth; have somebody to turn two tablespoonfuls of the mixture into the whites as soon as beaten enough, and which you mix with the egg-beater, then turn the rest or the mixture in, mixing gently with the wooden spoon. This must be done rather quickly, to prevent the whole from turning liquid. Put the mixture in the pastry-bag with tin tube No. 1 at the end of it, squeeze it out in sticks about four inches long into a baking-pan slightly buttered and dusted with flour, or on a piece of paper placed in the bottom of the pan; then dust them with sugar, and bake in a rather slow oven. They must not change in the oven, that is, they must not spread or swell, showing that the oven is too hot or too slow, or that the mixture has not been properly prepared. They must be like small sticks, round on the upper side and flat underneath. They are sometimes called *biscuits à la cuiller*. They are used to make a *Charlotte Russe*, or eaten with wine.

Cakes.—*Almond.*—Blanch, skin, and pound well one ounce of sweet almonds and the same of bitter ones, which you mix with eight ounces of pulverized sugar, six of flour, two eggs, a tablespoonful of brandy or rum, and a pinch of sugar. When thoroughly mixed, add five yolks of eggs, mix and stir for five minutes, then add also and mix half a pound of melted butter. Turn the mixture in small moulds, well buttered, and bake in a rather slow oven. Some almonds cut in small pieces may be spread over just before baking; or, when baked, some icing may be spread over. Serve cold. This is also called *Nantais cake*. Instead of almonds, use filberts, hazel-nuts, currants, peanuts, or raisins.

Fourré.—This is made with puff-paste and cream, or puff-paste and different mixtures placed inside of it, such as *Pithiviers cake* and fruit-pies.

Anchovy.—Knead four ounces of flour with two ounces of butter, a little salt, and a little water. Clean four anchovies and put them in vinegar for five minutes; then cut them in small pieces, put them in a bowl, and cover them with sweet-oil; leave them thus ten minutes. Roll the paste thin, then place a little more than half of it on a tart-dish, raising it all around with the thumb and forefinger; cover the paste with the anchovies, and these with the remainder of the paste, after having cut it in square pieces; spread some of the oil in which were the anchovies on it, bake in a warm oven, baste now and then with a little of the oil, and serve warm.

Apple.—Stew eight or ten apples and mash them through a sieve. Put them in a saucepan with about two ounces of butter and eight of sugar, set on the fire for five minutes, take off, let cool, and then mix with it five or six eggs, one after another. Turn the mixture into a buttered mould, which you place in a pan of boiling water, then boil slowly about half an hour, turn over a dish, and serve warm or cold.

Hard.—Put half a pound of flour on the paste-board and make a hole in the middle; put into it three ounces of pulverized sugar, three ounces of butter, two eggs, a pinch of cinnamon, a few drops of essence, and knead the whole well, dust the board with flour, roll the paste down to a thickness of about one-fourth of an inch, cut it in pieces with a paste-cutter, of any shape; beat one egg with a teaspoonful of sugar and glaze the pieces with it; with a piece of wood draw leaves or flowers on each, and bake in an oven at about 360 degrees Fahr. They are eaten cold at tea.

Heavy or Gâteau de Plomb.—Proceed as above with one pound of flour, a pinch of salt, one ounce of sugar, four yolks of eggs, one pound of butter, half a pint of cream; when rolled down as above, fold in two or four, and roll down again; repeat the process four times. Then place it in a bakepan and put in a hot oven. Serve cold at tea.

Milanais.—Put one pound of flour on the paste-board and make a hole in the middle, in which you put half a pound of butter, same of sugar, two eggs, a pinch of salt, and a quarter of a gill of rum. Mix and knead to a rather stiff dough with cold water. Spread it and roll it down to a thickness of about one-eighth of an inch. Glaze it with egg, dust with sugar and bake in a rather quick oven. When cold, cut it in two, spread some *compote* of peaches or of apricots on one half, put the other half over it, cut in pieces according to fancy, and serve.

Rum Cakes.—These are made with sponge cake cut with a paste-cutter, some sweetmeats or jelly is placed on the middle, then it is dusted with pulverized sugar, watered with rum, and then placed in the oven for about two minutes. These cakes have several names, according to the kind of sweetmeat used.

Savarin.—Put one pound of flour on the paste-board and make a hole in the middle; put into it four ounces of sugar, and make a hole again; then put in the middle four eggs, twelve ounces of butter, one and a half gills of milk; mix and knead the whole well; then mix again in the whole four ounces of leaven prepared as directed; butter a mould, dust it with sweet almonds chopped; put the mixture in it; put in a warm place (about 78 degrees Fahr.) to rise, and bake in an oven at 430 degrees Fahr. It will take about two and a half hours to rise. The mould must not be filled, else it will run over in rising.

Sauce for Savarin.—Put four ounces of sugar and half a pint of cold water in a block-tin saucepan, set it on the fire and boil till reduced about one-third; then add from one-half to one gill of rum (according to taste), give one more boil, and turn over the cake. Baste the cake with the sauce till the whole is absorbed by it. Serve warm or cold.

Sponge Cake.—Mix well together in a bowl six yolks of eggs with four ounces of sugar; add four ounces of flour and mix again, add also a few drops of essence, then whisk six whites of eggs to a stiff froth and mix them again with the rest. Butter a mould, put the mixture into it, not filling it more than two-thirds full, and bake in an oven at about 320 degrees. Sponge cake may be cut in pieces and used to make a *Charlotte Russe*, instead of lady's fingers.

Apple Dumplings.—Quarter, peel, and core the apples, and cut them in pieces, then envelop them in puff-paste with beef-suet, boil till thoroughly done, and serve warm with sugar, or with apple or wine sauce. It may also be served with sauce for puddings.

Buckwheat Cakes.—Make a kind of thin dough with tepid water, yeast, buckwheat flour, and a little sugar and salt, let rise, and fry with butter. Serve hot with sugar, or molasses, or butter.

Corn Cakes.—Mix well in a bowl two eggs with two ounces of melted butter, a pint of corn-meal, salt and sugar to taste. While mixing set milk on the fire, and as soon as it rises, turn it into the mixture, little by little, stirring and mixing the while, and till it makes a kind of thick dough. Butter well a shallow bakepan, put the mixture into it, and bake.

Crullers.—Mix well together and work with a wooden spoon, in a bowl, one egg with two ounces of melted butter and half a pound of pulverized sugar; then add salt, cinnamon, nutmeg, a few drops of essence, and one pound of flour, and mix again; add also milk, little by little, stirring and mixing at the same time, enough to make a thick batter. Divide the mixture in parts and fry in hot fat. (*See* Frying.)

Doughnuts.—Mix well together in a bowl four eggs with half a pound of sugar, add two or three ounces of melted butter and mix again, then mix with the whole, about one pound of flour and boiled milk enough to make a rather thick dough, season and mix well with the whole, nutmeg, cinnamon, and a few drops of essence. Cut in fancy pieces with a knife or paste-cutter, and fry in hot fat. (*See* Frying.) Dust with sugar, and serve hot.

Muffins.—Mix well together on the paste-board one pound of flour and three eggs, then add and mix again milk enough to make a thin dough, a little yeast and salt. Put away to rise; divide in parts and bake.

Pound Cake.—Take a large bowl and put in it one pound of melted butter and one pound of pulverized sugar, and mix the two thoroughly together with a wooden spoon; then add and mix well also with them, three eggs previously beaten with a saltspoonful of nutmeg and cinnamon, half of each. When the eggs are mixed, add also half a pound of flour, mix well again; then add six well-beaten eggs, and mix; then another half pound of flour, a few drops of essence of rose, half a gill of Sherry wine, a liquor-glass of brandy, four ounces of citron, and half a pound of comfited fruit, chopped fine. Beat and mix as well as possible. Butter a mould, dust it with fine bread-crumbs, turn the mixture into it, and bake in a warm but not quick oven. It takes about two and a half hours to bake. As soon as cold, serve it. It may be glazed with sugar, or sugar and white of egg.

Short Cake.—Cut puff-paste, made with a pound of flour and six or eight ounces of butter, in square or round pieces, bake; when cold, spread sweetened strawberries on, then cover with another cake, spread strawberries again on it, etc. Strawberry-jelly may be used.

Plum.—Mix well in a vessel a pound of sugar with a pound of butter, and then again with eight eggs, one at a time, also half a pound of raisins, half a pound of flour, a little rum, and a little yeast. Line a mould with buttered paper, turn the mixture into it, not filling it more than two-thirds full, place it in a warm but not quick oven for nearly two hours, remove the mould, and serve hot or cold.

Tea Cake.—Put half a pound of flour on the paste-board, and in the middle of it a pinch of salt, half an ounce of sugar, two eggs, four ounces of melted butter, and cold water enough to make a rather stiff paste. Knead well, roll down to about a quarter of an inch in thickness; cut it in pieces with a knife or paste-cutter; moisten the top with water by means of a brush, dust with sugar, and bake in an oven at about 370 degrees Fahr. Serve cold.

Viennois.—Make some biscuits in boxes, and when cold, cut off a little piece on the top, in the centre, which place you fill with peaches or apricots in *compote*; put two together; serve cold.

With Jelly.—Proceed as above in every particular, using currant or raspberry jelly instead of *compote*.

MEAT-PIES.

Pâtés de Viande.—Meat-pies are made in moulds without bottoms and which open in two, or are made of two pieces joined and fastened together with two pieces of wire. The size of the mould and that of the pie are according to taste. A pie may be made and filled with a reed-bird, or with a quail, or a partridge, or prairie-chicken, or with a dozen of them. We will give the receipt for one prairie-chicken.

Pâté of Game.—Bone a prairie-chicken as directed for birds, and cut it in about half a dozen slices or pieces. Grease the mould with butter and put it in a baking-pan. Put one pound of flour on the paste-board and make a hole in the middle; place in it six ounces of butter, one egg, a pinch of salt, and about one gill and a half of cold water, and knead the whole well. Roll it down to a thickness of about one-quarter of an inch, and of a rectangular shape; fold in two, and roll down again. Repeat this from six to twenty times; that is, till the paste is soft. The last time roll it down to a thickness of one-third of an inch, and give it as round a shape as possible. Dust the upper side slightly with flour, fold in two in this way: turn the side farthest from you on the other, so that the side of the paste nearest to you will be somewhat round, and the opposite one will be straight. By pulling with the hands the two ends of the straight side toward you, it will make it somewhat round also; then, take hold of the paste exactly in the places where you were pulling; put it in the mould with the side nearest to you on the top; open it gently, and with the hands spread it so that the bottom and sides of the mould will be perfectly lined with it. With a sharp knife cut the paste even with the top of the mould. Line the sides of the paste with thin slices of fat salt pork. Mix in a bowl one pound and a half of sausage-meat with two eggs, salt, pepper, a pinch of cinnamon and one of nutmeg; place a layer of this mixture about half an inch thick on the bottom of the paste; then a layer of thin slices of fat salt pork; one of slices of prairie-chicken; again a layer of sausage-meat, one of salt pork, etc., layer upon layer, till the mould is nearly full, finishing with a layer of sausage-meat, and giving to the top of the *pâté* a convex form, but leaving a space of about half an inch unfilled all around, so that the top of the *pâté* will be about one inch higher than the sides, and half an inch higher than the sides of the mould and paste. The cover of the *pâté* is made with the same paste as the bottom and sides, or with puff-paste.

Roll the paste down to a thickness of about one-eighth of an inch. Glaze the sides of the paste in the mould with egg; that is, the space (half an inch) left unfilled; put the paste for the cover on the *pâté*; press it gently against the other paste with the fingers in order to cause the two pastes to adhere; with a sharp knife cut off the paste even with the mould. Make a hole in the middle and on the top of the cover about one inch in diameter; cut five pieces of paste about three inches square, dust them slightly with flour; place them one upon another on your left thumb, keeping it erect; then with the right hand take hold of the pieces, bringing the edges together so that the top will form a ball; with a sharp knife make two cuts across and through the five pieces; form a kind of stem as if you were to imitate a mushroom with these pieces, and plant the stem in the hole; when baked it looks like a flower. Glaze the cover with egg; cut strips of paste in different shapes with a knife or paste-cutter, place them on it according to fancy, and bake in an oven at about 390 degrees Fahr. The strips of paste may also be glazed with egg. It will take about two hours to bake. As soon as cold, cut the cover all around and remove it; fill the empty places with meat or calf's-foot jelly and put it on the dish. Chop some of the same jelly, put some all around it and on the top; cut some of it also in fancy shapes with a knife or paste-cutter; place it all around the dish and on the top of the *pâté*, and serve.

The cut following represents a plain pie; that is, without any decoration, and immediately after having removed the mould.

Another, or Rabbit-Pie.—Chop very fine and separately one pound of veal, one of beef, one of lean fresh pork, three of rabbit or hare, and three of fat fresh pork. Mix the whole well together and season with salt, pepper, cinnamon, cloves, and nutmeg, all grated or in powder. Line a mould with paste as directed above, put a layer of the mixture in the mould about one inch thick, place on it slices of truffles, if handy and liked; then another layer, truffles, etc., till the mould is full. If filled without truffles, it is not necessary to put layer after layer. Cover also as above, and bake in a moderately heated oven, about 320 degrees Fahr. It takes from five to six hours to bake.

Another, or Prairie-chicken Pie.—Skin a prairie-hen (or several) and bone it. It is not necessary in boning it for a pie to proceed as directed for boned turkey, but merely to remove all the bones in the easiest and quickest manner; you cannot spoil the flesh, as it is to be chopped. Weigh the flesh when free from bones and skin. Weigh as much of each of the following: ham, salt pork, and calf's liver. Grate the salt pork and chop the three others very fine, and then pound the whole. Season with salt, pepper, cloves and nutmeg, both grated, a pinch of cinnamon and chopped parsley; mix with the whole two or three eggs, one at a time, in order to mix better. Line a mould with paste as directed above; line the paste with thin slices of salt pork, fill it with the mixture, and cover, bake, finish, and serve exactly the same as the preceding. For two prairie-hens it will require about three hours to bake. Slices of truffles may also be used; they are mixed at the same time with the eggs and seasonings.

With Cold Meat.—When the paste is placed in the mould as directed above, line it with thin slices of salt pork, then put a very thin layer of sausage-meat, prepared also as above, then fill with butcher's meat, poultry, and game, having previously removed all the bones, and cut the meat in strips; the greater the variety, the better the *pâté*. Put a little of each kind of meat used in a mortar, say from one ounce to a pound, with parsley, thyme, bay-leaf, salt and pepper; pound the whole well and then mix with one egg, half a gill of white wine, or a liquor-glass of brandy, to every pound of meat. Fill the hollow places with the mixture, to which you may add a little gravy or broth if it is not liquid enough. Place thin slices of salt pork on the top, cover with paste as described above, cook and serve as above also.

Meat-pies, as seen above, are made with every kind of meat; with one or several kinds at the same time, according to taste.

Wines and liquors may be used, it is only a matter of taste. The cover may be placed with only a hole in the centre, instead of decorating it.

By using in turn butcher's meat, poultry, and game, an infinite number of different *pâtés* can easily be made.

Terrines (Terreen, or Tureen).—A terrine differs from a meat-pie in this, that instead of using a tin or brass mould and lining it with paste, a *terrine* (French word for terreen) is used, and is only lined with thin slices of salt pork, and closed with its cover. It is filled, cooked, and served in the same way as a meat-pie.

Timbale.—The name *timbale* is given to a meat-pie when made in a straight tin mould, lined as a *terrine,* and covered with a tin cover. A *terrine* or *timbale* keeps longer in winter than the pie.

Pains de Gibier (Pains of Game).—This means, loaves of game. It is a *terrine* made with any kind of game, of one or of several kinds, with the exception that birds are boned and filled (*see* DIRECTIONS FOR BONING), before placing them in the terreen; also, before covering the terreen, place a piece of buttered paper all around, so as to have it as nearly air-tight as possible when covered. Bake as above, and as soon as out of the oven remove the cover; put a piece of tin, sheet-iron, or wood on the top, large enough to cover the meat, but not the border of the terreen. Place some weight on it in order to press the meat down, and leave thus over night. The weight and piece of tin are removed, the terreen is wiped clean, the cover placed on it, and it is then served, or served on a dish. It keeps very well in winter time, and many are imported from Europe, especially those made like the following:

Another.—Cut four ounces of boiled beef-tongue and one pound of truffles in large dice. Put about two ounces of salt pork in a frying-pan on the fire, and when fried, add about six ounces of the flesh of prairie-hen, cut in pieces, four prairie-hens' and four chicken livers, eight in all; stir, and when turning rather brown, add also chopped parsley, salt, and pepper; stir again for two or three minutes, and take off. Put in a mortar one pound of flesh of prairie-hen, baked and chopped; one pound and a quarter of fat salt pork, and about four ounces of *panade.* Pound the whole well and put it in a large bowl. Then pound well also the six ounces of prairie-hen flesh and eight livers with twelve yolks of eggs and a wine-glass of Madeira wine, and put in the bowl also. Add to it the tongue and truffles, and mix the whole well, adding game-gravy, or meat-gravy if more handy, about a gill of it, season to taste with salt, pepper, nutmeg, and cloves, grated. Bay-leaf and thyme, well pounded, may also be used, if liked. After being pounded, the whole may be mashed through a sieve, but it is really not necessary. Then place the mixture in one, two, or three *terrines,* cook, and serve as above.

Another.—Take the flesh of six prairie-hens when cooked, and pound it well. Pound also eight livers, fried; four of prairie-hens and four of chickens; put flesh and livers in a saucepan with gravy, set on a slow fire, and as soon as warm, add to it, little by little, and stirring continually, about three-fourths of its volume of good butter. When all the butter is in, take from the fire, mix one pound of truffles cut in dice with it; put the mixture in one or more terrines; cover, bake, and serve as above.

Terrines and *pains* are sometimes made with poultry, and in the same way as those of game.

Fish-Pies.—These are made in the same way as meat-pies, using cooked fish instead of meat, but putting fish only inside of the paste. When done it is filled with *coulis of fish* instead of jelly. Serve as a meat-pie. The fish must be free from bones.

Fruit-Pies.—Pies are made with paste and fruit or vegetables. The under-paste may be made of trimmings of puff-paste, or of the paste hereafter described, but the top is always made of puff-paste. The paste on the top may cover the fruit entirely, or it may be only strips running across, according to taste and fancy. The fruit is used raw or cooked previously, according to kind; if it requires longer cooking than the paste, or if it requires to be mixed or mashed, it must be cooked previously.

Under-Paste.—Put one pound of flour on the paste-board with six ounces of butter in the middle of it; also two ounces of sugar, two eggs, and cold water enough to make an ordinary paste, neither too stiff nor too soft. Roll the paste down to a thickness of one-eighth of an inch, spread it on a tin dish or bakepan, buttered slightly, raise the borders a little or place a strip of puff-paste all around it; put the fruit in the middle, then cover with a thin piece of puff-paste or place strips of it only over the fruit, and bake in a rather quick oven, about 390 degrees Fahr. The strips of paste are cut with a paste-cutter (caster-like) and placed across; one strip may also be placed all around. When trimmings of puff-paste are used for the under-paste, when placed on the tin or bake-pan, prick it in about a dozen places with a fork to prevent it from rising. To place a border around the paste, you have only to cut a strip of it about half an inch wide, wet the paste with water by means of a brush, that is, the edge or place where you are going to put it; then take hold of the strip, place one end of it on the paste and run it all around till you meet the end, cut it off and stick the two ends together by wetting them also. When the border is placed, then put the fruit in the middle; if the fruit is not cooked, it must be mixed with sugar and essence, or cinnamon, or nutmeg, according to kind, if cooked, that is, stewed, or in *compote* or in jelly, it is sweetened and flavored.

The following are used to make pies: *apples, apricots, cherries, currants, blackberries, cranberries, gooseberries, grapes, mulberries, oranges, peaches, pears, pine-apples, plums, quinces, raspberries, lemon, rhubarb, prunes, whortleberries,* etc. It is better to stone the fruit before using it. Pies are decorated in the three following ways:

1. When you use cooked fruit, put a thin layer of rice (prepared as for *croquettes*) on the paste, then a layer of stewed fruit; then the strips over, and bake. Two or three layers of each may be used.

2. When baked, spread over the pie some syrup of apples, of pears, or syrup for *compotes*.

3. Just before serving, spread some *crème légère* on the top, tastefully and fancifully, by means of a paper funnel, or with the pastry-bag.

Tarts and Tartelettes.—These are small pies. Instead of using a tin dish or a bakepan, you use small tin moulds, such as for *madeleines*, and proceed exactly as for pies.

Mince-Pie.—Every thing used to make a mince-pie is chopped fine, and the spices are used in powder. Prepare paste as directed for meat-pies, and make it either with or without mould. Proportions: to three pounds of beef add six pounds of beef-suet, one pound of currants, one of prunes, one of raisins, and one of apples, the rind of two lemons, two ounces of citron, and one pound of any kind of comfited fruit; nutmeg, mace, cinnamon, cloves, and sugar to taste; also wine or brandy, or both, to taste. Bake in a moderately heated oven. The fruits may be used candied or fresh, the apples fresh or dried, it is a matter of taste. Twenty kinds of fruits and meat may be used as well as three or four; there are no rules to make a mince-pie, since its compounds are not used to be tasted at all separately, but as a whole.

Pot-Pie.—Make a paste with one pound of flour, two ounces of butter, two ounces of beef-suet (the latter prepared as directed for puff-paste), a little salt and water, enough to make a rather stiff paste; roll it down to a thickness of about a quarter of an inch and fold it in three and roll down again; repeat the process half a dozen times, the last time leaving it rolled down and of the thickness above mentioned. Line the sides of a pot with it, lay slices or strips of salt pork on the bottom of the pot, then fill it with strips of meat, any and every kind (slices of potatoes may be added, if liked); season with salt, pepper, nutmeg, and cinnamon; fill with water or broth; cover with some of the same paste; cover the pan and boil gently till done. When the cover of paste is laid on, make a hole in the centre to let the steam out, and to fill up with water or broth if it boils away. Run a sharp-pointed knife or a skewer through, to ascertain when done. Serve warm. Proceed as above either for butcher's meat, chicken, and other domestic fowls, or game.

PUDDINGS.—Puddings are made of several materials and in a hundred different ways. Some are cooked by boiling, others are baked, and some are both boiled and baked. Puddings for inhabitants of cities ought to be made as light as possible. For persons working outside and at manual labor, it does not matter, because their food passes through the system in a short time. It is very well known that the poorer class of Americans eat too much pudding and pie. Many do it for economy, others for convenience. The former are mistaken, and the latter are blamable. Puddings and pies cost more in the end than meat properly and carefully prepared. We do not mean to do away with them entirely, but we advise every one to do with puddings as with every thing else, "use, but do not abuse." "Pies, cakes, and sweetmeats, are universally known to be poisoning to children, and the mothers who give them are conscious that they are purchasing the momentary smile of satisfaction at the risk of after-sickness, and perhaps of incurable disease."—PETER PARLEY.

The above needs no commentary; we only recommend it to the consideration of young mothers.

For Convenience.—We have taken the trouble to put questions about it to over three hundred mothers, wives of mechanics or of employés at a comparatively small salary, and we are sorry to say, that more than ninety per cent. gave us about the same answer—they make and cook cakes in one day, enough to feed the whole family for three days, to save the trouble of cooking every day. We cannot see where the trouble can be for a good wife and mother to prepare her husband and children's dinner.

Pudding-eating is an English custom; but, before following a custom of another country, people ought to consider if that custom or fashion (whatever it is) has not been introduced into that country by necessity, which is the case of pudding-eating in England and in some parts of Holland.

In England, where the fog is nearly perpetual, the stomach requires to be filled with something heavy, something that will stay there till the next meal, and very often longer than that.

It is well known that in England farm hands, or other persons working in the open air, eat six times a day, and have pudding at least three times; they drink home-brewed beer, which is very heavy, and very rich also. Let anyone here, in this pure, clear atmosphere, eat six times a day, have pudding three times, with a pint of home-brewed beer every time, and see how he will feel in the evening. We beg all, who may doubt our observations, to try the experiment.

Pastry in general, no matter how light it may be made, lies heavier on the stomach than any other food, and is very difficult of digestion. There are thousands of persons that have never had any indigestion but of pastry. Children like pastry very much; this is easily understood; as their young stomachs digest very rapidly, they crave food oftener than grown persons. Pastry being easier to have at any time than any thing else, it is given to them; and from habit in youth arises the liking when grown up. The stomach, being accustomed to it from infancy, may digest it better, but it is always at the expense of the whole system; the stomach must work hard, too hard in digesting it; whence come dyspepsia, weakness, and finally consumption, or debility, or any other sickness of the same kind.

The cut below represents a pudding (any kind), made in a mould, scalloped, and hollow in the middle; any kind of mould may be used for puddings.

Bread-Pudding.—Soak half a ten-cent loaf in milk for about an hour, and squeeze it with the hands; place the bread in a bowl and mix well with it a gill of milk, three tablespoonfuls of sugar, one ounce of citron, cut rather fine, four ounces of raisins, four ounces of melted butter, four yolks of eggs. Then beat the four whites of the eggs to a stiff froth and mix them with the rest. Grease a mould well with butter, dust it with bread-crumbs, turn the mixture into it, and bake. The mould must not be more than about two-thirds full. About 400 degrees Fahr. is the proper heat for a bread-pudding. It takes about forty minutes to bake. Serve with a sauce for pudding, hot or cold, according to taste.

Cabinet Pudding.—A cabinet pudding is made in any kind of a mould and of any size, with sponge-cake or lady's fingers. Butter a mould well; if the butter is too firm, warm it so as to grease the mould better. Slice some citron and cut it in lozenges or of any other shape, according to fancy, and place tastefully on the bottom of the mould; place some raisins all around also. It is not necessary to cover the bottom with them, but have some here and there, imitating flowers, stars, etc. Then put over them a layer of sponge-cake, cut in strips of any length and about half an inch thick; on this layer place some citron, some comfited (candied) fruit of one or several kinds, and all cut in dice, also some raisins; then another layer of cake, some more fruit, and so on, till the mould is full. After having placed the citron and raisins on the bottom, it is not necessary to put the rest in with care or order, but merely fill the mould with them and so that they are all mixed up. Set about a pint of milk on the fire and take it off as soon as it rises. Mix well in a bowl three ounces of sugar with three yolks of eggs, then turn the milk into the bowl, little by little, stirring and mixing the while, and pour the mixture over the cake, fruit, etc., into the mould. The above quantities of milk, sugar, and eggs are for a middling-sized pudding, and it will be very easy to make more or less, according to the size of the pudding. The mixture must be poured over in sprinkling, and it must nearly cover the whole within about half an inch. It must not be poured too slowly, for, the cake absorbing the liquor pretty fast, you would have too much of it if you were filling as directed above; we mean filling till the mould is nearly full. Place the mould in a pan of cold water so that it is about one-third covered by it, set on the fire, and as soon as it boils, place the whole, pan and mould, in an oven at about 380 degrees Fahr., and bake. For a middling-sized one it takes about one hour. When done, place a dish over the mould, turn upside down, remove the mould, and serve with a sauce for puddings.

With Vermicelli.—Blanch four ounces of vermicelli, drain and drop it in cold water and drain again. While the vermicelli is cooking, put about a quart of milk in a saucepan on the fire with two ounces of sugar and a piece of lemon-rind, stir now and then to dissolve the sugar, and as soon as the milk rises, take it from the fire, remove the lemon, then turn the vermicelli into it, put back on the fire, add a tablespoonful of butter, stir continually, and when the vermicelli is well cooked, take off, mix well with the whole four eggs and sugar to taste. Turn the mixture into a well-buttered mould, place it in a pan of boiling water, boil slowly for ten minutes, then place as it is, pan and mould, in a moderately-heated oven to finish the cooking. It will take from fifteen to twenty minutes. Proceed as above with *macaroni*, *tapioca*, etc.

Plum-Pudding.—Break with the hands, in small pieces, about twelve ounces of the soft part of good and well-baked bread, not too fresh, but not stale, and grate it. Clean twelve ounces of raisins and currants, half of each. Cut in small dice four ounces of citron and four ounces of candied orange-rind. Chop fine the rind of a lemon. Butter a towel slightly and dust it with flour, slightly also. Take twelve ounces of good fresh beef-suet, remove the fibres and skin as well as possible, and chop it rather fine with three or four ounces of flour, and which put in a large bowl. Mix with it seven eggs and half a pound of sugar. It is believed by many that brown sugar is better than white, but it is only a belief, if not a prejudice. Add and mix again the bread, the raisins, and currants, the citron, and orange-rind. Having the whole thoroughly mixed, add half a gill of French brandy or Jamaica rum, a little salt, the lemon-rind, half a gill of cream or a little milk, and a little grated cinnamon. Place the mixture on the towel, and tie it as fast as possible, giving it a round shape. Drop the towel in boiling water, and boil for from four to five hours. Some boil a plum-pudding as long as seven hours. It may also be boiled in a mould for that purpose, but it is easier in a towel and quite as good. When taken from the water, remove the towel, cut a little piece of the pudding off to make it stand better on the dish. The place cut off is generally where the towel was tied, being the less smooth. The cut following shows a plum-pudding boiled in a towel.

Serve with a sauce for puddings. The sauce may be served in a boat, or spread all over the pudding. When served the second day, or cold for supper, it is cut in slices; some Jamaica rum is poured over it, then set on fire, basting as long as it burns, and serve. It is generally burnt on the table, but the rum may be poured over in the kitchen. The cut below represents a whole one with rum around it and on fire.

Biscottes.—Put half a pound of flour on the paste-board and make a hole in the middle of it; put in the hole four ounces of sugar, one ounce of butter, three yolks of eggs, and a few drops of essence to flavor the cakes. Mix and knead the whole well with the hand. When like dough, roll it under your hands and bring it to a rope-like form of about three-quarters of an inch in diameter; cut it in pieces about two inches long; roll again with the hand so as to make a ball of each; then roll again with both hands so as to give each piece a round, elongated, olive shape; that is, smaller at each end than at the middle. Put them in a baking-pan, greased with butter; glaze each piece well with egg and a little sugar beaten together, then, with a sharp knife, which you dip in flour, make a cut on the top and into each cake, lengthwise, about three-quarters through, and bake in an oven at 350 degrees Fahr. Serve cold. It is an excellent cake for tea as well as for dessert.

With Almonds.—Add to the above mixture one ounce of pounded almonds.

With Filberts or Hazel-nuts.—Add to the mixture for *biscottes*, one ounce of filberts or hazel-nuts, pounded well.

Brioche.—Mix together on the paste-board, one pound of flour, six eggs, one pound of butter, four ounces of leaven prepared as directed, and tepid water enough to make a rather soft dough, then beat well. The longer it is beaten the better, and the lighter the *brioche* will be. By beating we mean—take hold of the dough with the right hand, raise it and then throw it with force on the board and in the same place where it was; repeat that till it comes off your hand without any of the paste sticking to it. Put the mixture in a tin vessel, set it in a warm place (about 78° Fahr.) for about two hours to rise, and then put immediately on ice to cool. When cold, put it back on the paste-board, cut off about one-fourth of it. Make a kind of crown with the larger piece, but not a very large one; let the hole in the middle be about three inches in diameter. Then give the other piece a rope-like shape, about three-quarters of an inch in diameter; place it over the crown, giving it the shape of a star, and bake in an oven at 430°. Serve warm, without sauce.

Baba.—Mix together and beat as for a *brioche,* one pound of flour, ten eggs, one pound and a quarter of butter, four ounces of raisins, four ounces of citron, four ounces of leaven, about half a pound of different kinds of fruits, preserved in syrup or candied, all cut fine; put to rise, let cool, shape, bake and serve as a *brioche*.

A *baba* may be baked in a mould; the cut on the previous page represents one.

Croquignolles.—Put in a bowl four ounces of flour, a teaspoonful of sugar, a pinch of salt, half a pound of butter, four whites of eggs, and a few drops of essence; mix the whole well so as to make a very stiff paste. Then put the mixture on the paste-board, and roll it in a rope-like form about half an inch in diameter; then cut it in pieces about half an inch long, glaze with yolk of egg, dust with sugar, and bake in a warm but not quick oven. Serve cold at tea.

Galette.—Knead together half a pound of flour, six ounces of butter, two eggs, and a pinch of salt; roll it down to a thickness of a quarter of an inch, put in a bake-pan in the oven, and when nearly done, take off; mix well together one egg with a gill of cream and an ounce of butter, while the *galette* is in the oven, spread the mixture over it, put back in the oven, finish the cooking, and serve cold at tea.

Génoises.—Put in a large bowl six ounces of flour, eight of sugar, two eggs, a liquor-glass of brandy or rum, and a few drops of essence; mix and stir the whole well for three minutes, then add two more eggs, stir and mix one minute longer, add again four eggs and continue stirring one minute longer. Melt half a pound of butter in another bowl, and mix with it about two tablespoonfuls of the mixture; when, turn into the other bowl and mix the whole well together. Butter a bakepan, spread the mixture in it, and bake in a rather slow oven (about 300° Fahr.). When the top is well baked, turn it over and finish it. When cold, cut the whole in strips about two inches long, then again across so as to make pieces of a lozenge-shape, and serve as it is or with a *sauce for puddings*.

The same, with Almonds.—Pound well four or six ounces of sweet almonds, place them in the bowl with the rest, and then mix, bake, and serve as the above one.

Do the same with *bitter almonds, hazel-nuts, peanuts, filberts,* and *raisins*; flavor with any kind of essence.

With Chocolate.—When the cake is cut in pieces, glaze it as directed for *éclair au chocolat*.

With Sweetmeats.—When the cake is cut in pieces, with a sharp-pointed knife, cut off a part of each piece, on the top and right in the centre, so as to make a small hole, which you fill with any kind of sweetmeat or with any *cream,* and then serve. When thus served, they are called under several names.

Macaroons.—Throw into boiling water for five minutes ten ounces of sweet almonds, and two ounces of bitter ones; skin them well; put in a mortar, and pound them to a paste, adding a few drops of the white of eggs during the process. Grind well also a pound of white sugar, with the quarter of a rind of lemon well grated; then mix well together almonds, sugar, and the whites of two eggs. Make balls of any size with it; put the balls on a piece of paper, beat the yolk of an egg with half a gill of water, and glaze the top of the balls with it by means of a brush; put them in a slow oven; it will take about fifteen minutes to cook them.

Macaroons with Chocolate.—Melt on a slow fire and in a tin pan three ounces of chocolate without sugar (known as Baker's chocolate); then work it to a thick paste with one pound of pulverized sugar, and three whites of eggs. Roll the mixture down to a thickness of about one-quarter of an inch; cut it in small round pieces with a paste-cutter, either plain or scalloped; butter a pan slightly and dust it with flour and sugar, half of each, place the pieces of paste or mixture in and bake in a hot but not quick oven. Serve cold.

Madeleines.—Mix well together in a bowl three ounces of sugar, three of flour, and two eggs, then again one ounce of melted butter and a few drops of essence to flavor. Butter slightly small tin moulds, dust them slightly also with flour and sugar, half of each, turn the mixture in, filling the moulds only two-thirds full, and bake in an oven at about 340°. Serve cold.

The same, with Almonds.—Chop rather fine some sweet almonds, and when the mixture is in the moulds as described above, spread the almonds over them; bake, and serve as above.

Do the same with *hazel-nuts, filberts, peanuts,* or *raisins.*

Meringues or Kisses.—Put half a pound of pulverized sugar in a plate, beat six whites of eggs to a stiff froth as directed, then have somebody to sprinkle the half pound of sugar into the eggs, and while you are still beating, which must be done in two seconds; stop beating and mix gently with a spoon, not by stirring but by turning the whole upside down several times. If it is stirred too much, it may turn too liquid. Put the mixture in the pastry-bag, with tin tube No. 2 at the end of it; spread the mixture on paper in a baking-pan, in oblong cakes about three inches long; dust them with pulverized sugar, and put in an oven at from 220° to 230° Fahr. It requires some time to dry them, about one hour. As soon as taken from the oven, place one in your left hand, the top downward; press gently on the under side which is up, with the first finger of the right hand, so as to make a hollow; put in that hollow twice as much cream as is necessary to fill it; place another cake prepared alike over the cream; so that the two will be united and kept together by the cream; do the same with the rest; place them tastefully on a dish; dust them with sugar, and serve. They are generally filled with *whipped cream*, but may be filled with *crème légère* or *crème cuite*. They may also be filled with *crème Chantilly*.

Swiss Meringue.—Instead of squeezing the mixture out and spreading it in oblong cakes, make a crown of it, then another and another, four in all, dust and bake in the same way; place them on a dish, one above the other, and fill the middle of the dish with cream as above. Serve cold. The mixture may also be placed on paper by the spoonful, but they are not as sightly as by means of the pastry-bag.

Zephyrs.—Proceed as for meringues as far as mixing the sugar with the whites of eggs, when mix also with both a few drops of cochineal. Put the mixture in the pastry-bag, with tin tube No. 1 at the end of it. Squeeze the mixture out and spread it on paper in a baking-pan, in different shapes: dentilated, convoluted, overlapping, waved, etc., according to fancy, about three inches and a half long. Bake in same oven as meringues, and serve when cold, as they are.

Nougat.—Throw a pound of sweet almonds into boiling water for five minutes; skin them well, and when cool cut them in four or five pieces lengthwise; then melt a pound of fine white sugar with two spoonfuls of water, in a copper or crockery pan, and on a good fire, stirring all the time with a wooden spoon; when well melted, put the almonds in; keep stirring about five minutes longer, take from the fire, add a little of the rind of a lemon well grated, oil the mould, put it on the corner of the range in a warm but not too hot place; put the almonds and sugar in the mould, and little by little take off when of a brown color, turn on a plate, remove the mould, and serve.

Pancakes.—Make a thin paste with one pound of flour, four eggs, two tablespoonfuls of sweet-oil, one of French brandy, a little salt, the necessary quantity of lukewarm water and milk, about half of each; let it remain thus two or three hours at least; then put about an ounce of lard, butter, or oil in a frying-pan, and set it on a brisk fire; when hot, put some of the paste in it with a ladle, spread the paste so as to cover the bottom of the pan; fry on both sides, place it on a dish, dust it with fine white sugar on both sides, and serve warm.

Buckwheat and other pancakes are made in the same way.

Waffles.—Make a thin paste with eight ounces of flour, six ounces of pulverized sugar, two eggs, a few drops of essence to flavor, half a liquor-glass of brandy or rum, and milk. Warm and butter both sides of the mould, put some of the paste into it, close it gently, set it on the fire, turn over to heat both sides equally, dust them with sugar when done, and serve either warm or cold. It takes hardly a minute for each with a good fire.

BREAD.

It is next to an impossibility to bake bread in a small oven; half the time the bread is too much or not enough baked. In cities, where good baker's bread can be bought, it comes as cheap as it can be made at home, if not cheaper, and saves a great deal of time and labor. It is not difficult to make good bread with good flour. There are several ways of making and of using yeast. Some are better than others; but many, though differently manipulated, bring about the same results. The only difficulty is the baking of it. Bakers can almost always bake bread properly, having large brick ovens. If they do not bake their bread enough, which is generally the case, it is not because they cannot, but because under-baked bread is heavier, and people, especially the poorer class, buy it in preference to the other; judging by the weight, they think they have more of it for a certain sum of money. Under-baked bread is difficult of digestion. (*See* Food.)

The best bread is made with the best wheat-flour, all that can be said by anybody to the contrary notwithstanding. Rye, corn, and barley bread are excellent, and may be partaken of by those whose constitution, occupation, etc., allow it. In every thing, bread included, the people, or what may be called "the million," are wiser than *soi-disant* philosophers; and if oat-meal or Indian-meal were better than wheat-flour, they would be dearer. To describe or discuss the innumerable methods of making bread would require several volumes. We have perused carefully hundreds of them; they nearly all differ theoretically, but practically, when practical (which is not always the case), they amount to about the same thing. We think that the only difficulty, if difficulty there be, is in the use of the yeast, the making of the same, and the baking. Chemical processes for rising will never equal the processes of nature and time. Many bakers do not use the yeast properly, their bread being sour or musty; some sweeten their bread, to disguise an inferior quality of flour, or as an antidote to sourness or mustiness.

Bread gets dry after a while, and is inferior in quality and taste. The lighter the bread the better, although many do not think so. The belief may come from the fact that the lighter bread is the more porous, and therefore the quicker it evaporates and loses its taste. Warm bread, besides being injurious to the teeth, is difficult of digestion. When perfectly cold, let it stand in a dry place, neither cold nor warm, for one or two hours, and use. We give below the best methods of making bread—French bread, or rather good light bread, for we do not see that it is more French than Chinese or American, as long as it can be made everywhere with good flour; it is certainly the best for inhabitants of a large city, and especially for those having a sedentary occupation. Let us apply the proverb to bread as well as to every thing else: "Feed me with food convenient for me."—*Bible*.

Mix well together one gill of good strong yeast with half a pound of flour, so that it makes a rather stiff paste. Knead so that you shape it like a ball. Make two cuts with a knife on the top, across and about one-quarter of an inch deep; then place the paste in a bowl of tepid water (milk-warm), the cuts upward. After it has been in the water for a few minutes it will float and swell; let it float about two minutes, when take off and use. Put six ounces of flour on the paste-board, and make a hole in the middle; put into it the yeast prepared as above, tepid water enough to make an ordinary dough, and salt to taste. Knead well, shape according to fancy, put in a warm place (about 78 deg. Fahr.) to rise, and bake. It requires about six hours to rise.

Another.—Wash and clean thoroughly half a pound of potatoes, and then steam them with the skins on. Mash them well with half a pint of flour, about half a pint of tepid water, and half an ounce of salt. When thoroughly mixed, put away in a warm place (about 78 deg. Fahr.) for one hour. Then add and mix with it half a pint of good yeast, and put away in the same place for about nine hours. It may take a little longer than nine hours or a little less, but it is very easy to know, and in this way: after a while it will rise slowly and gradually for some time, and then begin to fall; as soon as it begins to fall, mix a little tepid water with it and strain through a sieve; throw away potato skins and eyes; mix what is strained with two pounds of flour and tepid water enough to make an ordinary dough. Put it away again in the same place until it cracks on the top, which will take place in about an hour. Then put six pounds of flour on the paste-board, and make a hole in the middle; put into it a little tepid water and the dough when cracked; knead the whole well with water enough to make an ordinary dough, salt to taste. To knead it well, it is necessary to raise the dough or part of it, and then throw it back on the paste-board with force. The more the dough is kneaded, the better and lighter the bread. Then shape the loaves, let rise, and bake in a very quick oven.

To shape.—Divide the dough, as soon as kneaded, in as many parts as you wish to make loaves; then knead each part, one after another, so as to make a kind of ball; then, by rolling and pulling it, give it an elongated, sausage-like shape. A pound loaf can be made a foot and a half long, as well as four inches; it will only be narrower and thinner, and will have more crust. When the dough is thus elongated, take a round stick or a small rolling-pin, place it on the top of the dough, right on the middle, lengthwise, and then press on it and roll just a little, to and fro, so as to make a kind of furrow in the middle. Have a towel well dusted with flour, place the dough on it upside down, that is, the furrowed side under; let rise as ordinary bread; turn it into a pan, but so that the furrowed side will be up (the side that was down in rising must be up in baking); dust the furrow well with rye-flour to prevent the paste from closing, so that the top of the loaf will be concave instead of convex when baked.

Another.—Steam half a pound of potatoes and mash them well; then mix them immediately and while hot with about a pint of flour, a quart of water, and half a pint of good strong yeast. Leave the mixture six hours in a rather warm place, then strain through a sieve, pressing the potato-skins so as to squeeze all the liquid out of them. Immediately add to the strained mixture flour enough to make ordinary dough, which you knead a little, and let stand as it is from one to two hours and a half, according to temperature. Knead then with it about six pounds of flour, salt to taste, and tepid water to make ordinary dough, and leave it thus two hours, then shape in the same way as the above; put it to rise in the same way also (it will take from one to two hours, according to temperature); dust with rye-flour, and bake.

French bread may be shaped like other bread, round or square; it is just as good.

Rolls, or rather French rolls as they are generally called, are made, shaped, and baked in the same way.

It is a mistake to call *bread* certain mixtures of flour, soda, and milk; or flour, milk, and butter, etc.; it is no more bread than a mixture of carbonic acid, water, alcohol, molasses, vitriol, etc., is wine. No one can give a name to such a mixture except chemists.

BILLS OF FARE.

Dinner-Time.—On account of the various occupations of members of the same family, this is often the first and only time of the day that sees them all assembled. It is the dinner that mostly supplies the waste that the system has undergone for twenty-four hours. Being taken after the day's work is over, it gives to the stomach time to digest (mind and stomach never working at the same time). (*See* FOOD, ECONOMY, COFFEE, AND TEA.)

The dinner, being the most substantial meal of the day, requires more preparation than any other meal; the bill of fare of it should, therefore, be made the day before, or at least early in the morning. It should always be made between the mistress or master of the house and the cook; written and hung in the kitchen, near the clock. The first thing to put down is what may be left from the preceding day, and also what may be in the larder; then what is wanted in butcher's meat or poultry, or both; the fish or game, or both, and which, with vegetables, are according to the market. It is then one of the duties of the cook to make a list of what is wanted as accessories; such as flour, eggs, sugar, spices, etc.

Besides the above, it is also the duty of the cook to send the dishes to the table in their regular order; for, if the whole dinner is sent at once, all the dishes have to be eaten at once also, else the last get cold and are unpalatable, or, by mixing them, they are rendered tasteless, as the flavor of one neutralizes (if it does not destroy) the taste of another.

To make models of bills of fare is not difficult, but to follow them is nearly impossible; hardly one in a hundred would suit any one.

Bills of fare vary according to the season of the year, and therefore to the produce in the market.

We will try to give another, and we think a better way of making them to suit everybody, every purse, and at any time.

A dinner, no matter how grand, is composed of three courses, and seven kinds of dishes.

The first course comprises dishes of four kinds, viz.: potages, *hors-d'oeuvres, relevés, and entrées*.

The second course comprises dishes of two kinds, viz.: *rôts* and *entremets*.

The third course comprises dishes of one kind, the dessert.

The number of dishes of each kind is generally according to the number of guests.

It may also be according to the importance of the occasion for which the dinner is given; to the honor the giver or givers wish to show the personage or personages invited; to the amount of money they are willing to spend, etc.

The following table shows how many dishes of each kind are to be served at dinner to a certain number of persons:

For..	2	4	6	10	16	20	30	40	50	60	80	100	Persons.
Serve	1	1	1	2	2	2	4	4	4	6	8	8	Potages.
"	2	2	2	4	4	6	6	10	10	12	12	16	Hors-d'oeuvres.
"	1	1	1	2	2	2	4	4	4	6	8	8	Relevés of fish.
"	1	1	1	2	2	2	4	4	4	6	8	8	" of meat.
"	2	2	2	4	4	4	8	8	8	12	16	16	Entrées.
"	1	1	1	2	2	2	4	4	4	6	8	8	Rôts.
"	1	1	1	2	2	2	4	4	4	6	8	8	Salads of greens.
"	2	2	2	4	4	4	8	8	8	12	16	16	Entremets.
"					2	2	2	4	4	6		8	Large side pieces of Relevés & Entrées.
"						2	2	4	4	6			" cakes.
"	4	4	4	8	8	8	16	16	16	24	32	36	Plates of Dessert.

The above table shows the number of dishes, but more than one dish of the same kind can be served; for instance, four kinds of potages, *relevés*, etc., are served for forty; but two or four dishes of each kind can be served.

The size of the *relevés* and *rôts* should be according to the number of guests.

It is just as easy to select dishes for a small family-dinner as for a grand one; two, three, four, or more dishes can be selected; for instance, you select a potage, an *entrée* or *rôt*, or both, one vegetable or a sweet dish, or both; and one or as many plates of dessert as you please.

Have a bouquet on the middle of the table, if possible, or at least a basket of fruit. Flowers during dinner have the same effect as music after it; they soften the manners, and gently and sweetly gratify the senses.

To simplify and render the making of bills of fare easy, we have divided the different dishes into seven parts, each part being in the order the dishes of which must be served, and representing the seven kinds of dishes composing a dinner. By this means you select the dish or dishes which suit you, and which you can procure in any or all of the seven parts, and your bill of fare is made, and more to your liking than any steward on earth can do.

Order of dishes.—1. *Potages*. 2. *hors-d'oeuvres*. 3. *Relevés*: of fish, and then of meat. 4. *Entrées*: beef, mutton, lamb, veal, fish, poultry, and game last. 5. *Rôts*: of meat, and then of fish. 6. *Entremets*: salads of greens, vegetables, eggs, macaroni, sweet dishes, and cakes. 7. *Dessert*: cheese the first.

First part, or *Potages*.—Any kind coming under the head of potages or soups.

Second part, or *hors-d'oeuvres*.—These are small dishes placed on the table as soon as the soup-dish is removed or even before, and which are removed just before serving the sweet dishes of the *entremets*. They are passed round after every dish, on account of being considered more as appetizers, as repairers of the natural waste of animal life. Very little of them is partaken of at a time; they are *anchovies*; *artichockes*, raw; pickled *beets*; *butter*; *caviare*; *cervelas*; raw *cucumbers*; *figs*; every kind of *fish*, salted, smoked, pickled, or preserved in oil; every kind of *pickled fruit*; *horse-radish*; *horse-radish butter*; *melons*; broiled *mushrooms*; *olives*; raw and pickled *oysters*; steamed *potatoes* served with butter; *radishes* and butter; *sardines*;

saucissons; *sausages*, salt and smoked, but not fresh; salted and smoked *tongue*; *tunny, walnuts* in salad.

Third part, or *Relevés*.—*Relevés* are composed of fish and large pieces of meat. A fish served whole is always a *relevé*; in pieces, it is an *entrée*. Pieces of *beef, mutton*, and *pork*, roasted, are always served as *relevés*. At a family dinner the *relevé* is almost always a fish. The other pieces of meat that are served as *relevés* are: *bear, buffalo*, boiled and corned *beef, leg* and *saddle* of mutton, *quarters* of lamb, large pieces of *veal*; also all *vol-au-vent* of meat and of fish, *boucheés* and *fish-pies*.

Fourth part, or *Entrées*.—These comprise every dish of meat, except poultry and game, when roasted; every dish of *fish* not served whole; also *pâtés de foies gras, sour-krout, snails, meat-pies, terrines, pains* of game and of poultry. The dishes of *meat* mentioned in the *relevés* may be served as entrées at a family dinner. The order of the dishes is described above.

Fifth part, or *Rôts*.—*Poultry, game*, and *fish*. At a family dinner, *lamb* and *veal* are often served as roasted pieces, especially at seasons when there is no game, and poultry is scarce.

Sixth part, or *Entremets*.—The following are served as *entremets*: all *salads* of greens; all dishes of *vegetables*, of *omelets*, except four, viz., with bacon, salt pork, ham, and kidneys. Also dishes of *macaroni*, of *rice, eggs à la neige*, all *sweet dishes* (sweet dishes are also served as *dessert*), and *cakes*; such as *baba, brioche, génoises, madeleines, savarin*, and sponge-cake.

Seventh part, or *Dessert*.—The dessert comprises ripe *fruit, sweet dishes* (these are also served as *entremets*, according to taste), *pastry* (except meat-pies, *terrines*, and *pains*), *salads* of fruits, and cheese. The latter is always served the first (*see* CHEESE). After cheese, there is no rule for serving the other plates of dessert; it is according to each one's taste.

Punch is served after the *entrées* or after the *relevés* of fish, according to taste.

Early Breakfast.—We are of opinion that everybody ought to eat as little meat as possible, and drink no wine, beer, or any other liquor at an early breakfast, no matter what the sex or age may be, except when prescribed by the physician in case of sickness, debility, etc. The food may be selected from the following: *bread* and *butter*, *eggs*, *omelets*, fried *fish*, fried *vegetables*, *sardines*, and *fruit*, according to the season.

As for meat, in case it should be eaten, it ought to be cold, such as fowl or veal, cooked the day before.

Muffins, and other cakes or pastes, served warm, are very bad for the stomach and teeth.

The beverage ought to be either coffee, with milk, chocolate, cocoa, choca, or cold water, but do not by any means drink tea at breakfast; it is too astringent.

Although cold meat is not by far so injurious as warm meat for breakfast, it ought, nevertheless, to be as little partaken of as possible, and especially by the young.

Late Breakfast, Lunch, Tea, and early Supper.—At these meals the following dishes may be served:

Every dish served as a *hors-d'oeuvre*, *calf's* head and feet, bear *hams*, *head-cheese*, *eggs* cooked in any way, *omelets*, *mutton* chops, *veal* cutlets, fried *fish*, ripe *fruit*, boned *birds*, *ham*, cold *meat* of any kind, *oysters*, *pâté de foies gras*, *salads* of chicken, or any other birds, and of lobster, *sandwiches*, *sardines*, fried *vegetables*, *sweet dishes*, and *pastry*.

Late Supper.—This being the last meal taken before retiring, persons should be careful about what they eat then, especially those who take no bodily exercise, or retire soon after it. Some are not aware that their rest depends nearly, if not entirely, on what they have eaten at supper. The lighter the food the better; such as fried *fish, sardines, lait de poule, bavaroise*, well-ripened *fruit*, a *cream*, a little *iced fruit, fruit-jelly, prunes*, etc.

The gastronomical or hygienic rule to be observed in eating, it will be seen, is therefore, after the soup and *hors-d'oeuvres*, to commence with the heaviest or most substantial dishes, and to finish with the lightest. The rule is just the opposite for wines. Here we must commence with the lightest, and end with those which contain the most alcohol, and are consequently the heaviest.

www.ingramcontent.com/pod-product-compliance
Lightning Source LLC
Chambersburg PA
CBHW081122080526
44587CB00021B/3716